MW01296109

Puzzle Piece Heart

What I Learned While Single Parenting

Roxie Kaminski

Thank you to my children,
Kelly, Mike, Nick and Kathy Jane,
for making me a better me.

Table of Contents

FOREWORD

MIKE *born 1975*

My mother has been thinking about writing a book about parenting for quite some time. I think that like most aspiring writers, including myself, she has struggled with finding the confidence within herself to realize that not only is she creative enough to undertake such a project, but that she probably also has doubts as to whether or not she has the requisite knowledge to write about this particular subject. My older sister Kelly approached all of us with the idea of composing a foreword for my mom's book. After all, if anyone should judge whether or not a mom is capable of writing a book about parenting, who better than her four children? As is often the case with Kelly, I thought this was a great idea. But that is standard for Kelly – she is without a doubt the most creative and thoughtful person I have ever met. She is always thinking of others and is unbelievably giving of her time and energy. As for my other two siblings who wrote this foreword, they are incredible individuals in their own right. My brother, Nick, is a very successful and motivated construction engineer, and is the type of person that everyone should be lucky enough to have as a brother. He will do anything for anyone, and truly exemplifies the terms *friendship* and *family*. Just being in his presence brings a smile to my face. My baby sister Kathy is amazing. She is the most dedicated and hard-working individual that I have ever met. And at the same time she always puts her friends and family first, and has always been there for all of us when we need her.

As I approach the age at which I am starting to think about having a family, I am amazed at how many doubts and pressures I feel in regards to the responsibilities of parenting, and I am still three months short of my own wedding date. I sometimes feel like a bull rider must feel before an important ride – you know that it is going to be really exciting and difficult, and you just hope that you can hang on until the eight second buzzer. My tremendous excitement in regards to being a parent is tempered by constant doubts as to whether or not I will be able to be a good father to my future children.

Although I am nervous about being a father, I know I have been extraordinarily blessed. I, along with my three siblings, have the best mom in the world. Now this is a claim that many people make, and yet I know that I am right. My mom is a woman who grabbed the reins of parenting and didn't just make it to the buzzer – she turned the bull into a friendly old lap dog. Not only is she a wonderful mom, she is an amazing person and my best friend. I could probably write an entire novel as to why I feel my mom is the perfect person to write a book about parenting, but I think that one story in particular really indicates the type of person that she is...

The howling wind caused all of us to sit as close together as we possibly could on the frigid metal bench of the visitor's dugout. It was the second game of the first double header of the year for my high school baseball team, and northern Illinois spring weather had reared her ugly head. The weather had started out reasonably enough, with the temperature somewhere in the mid 30's, and a moderate breeze blowing. Certainly not ideal baseball weather, but it could have been worse. And then it got worse – much worse. Over the course of the first game, the temperature began to steadily decline, as the wind speed started rising. By the break in between games, many of the fans had given up and headed for home. I do not recall which team won the first game, but I do remember watching the fans heading home while we warmed up for the second game, and thinking that I wished I was heading for home, as well. But of course we didn't have that option.

I don't ever recall a sporting event in which the players had less interest in the score, than in just finishing the game so that everyone could go home and defrost. By the third inning everyone not actually playing in the field or batting was scrunched together on the bench, staring at the dugout floor, and praying that the game would end soon. By the fourth inning I could no longer feel my feet, and by the fifth inning I wanted to be lit on fire. It was that cold. At this point, it had dropped into the low 20's, and the wind was howling. They had to be gusting close to 45 miles per hour. The wind chill, if I remember correctly, was in single digits. It was by far the coldest I had ever been in a sporting event. The entire team was miserable. Conversation had long since ceased as all of us on the bench daydreamed about what it felt like to be warm – or at least tried to remember the last time we had had a semblance of feeling in our extremities. It was at this point that the silence was broken by my good friend, Greg, who was seated next to me on the bench.

"Oh. My. God. Who in the world is still here watching the game?"

It took a second for me to realize that he was talking about a fan still watching the game from the bleachers, and then it hit me.

That has to be my mom.

I looked out at the bleachers, and sure enough, there she was. The home bleachers were completely barren, and across the field on the visitor bleachers sat one lone individual, bundled up in her winter coat with a Strawberry Shortcake sleeping bag unzipped and draped over her shoulders. My mom. After all of the other parents had long since given in to the elements, my mom remained as the sole fan strong enough to bear the weather and offer her support. I walked over to her to see what in the world was wrong with her, and tell her that she should go home and warm up. She looked at me, smiled and asked who would support my teammates and me if she left? And that, in a nutshell, is my mom.

* * * * *

KATHY *born 1980*

People are often shocked when I say that my mom is my best friend, but once you read this book you'll begin to understand why. She is not only my best friend, but also the best mother I could have asked for, and the best human being I know. Her compassion, wit, strength, confidence, and love are evident to anyone who has the opportunity to know her. When she told me she was writing a book about raising my siblings and me, I selfishly thought of how lucky my brothers and sister and I would be to have the stories of our childhood and young adult lives recorded for years to come. But this book is much more than that. Everyone can take something away from reading it, whether it makes you laugh or cry, teaches you something about yourself or the person you want to be. Roxie is an inspiration to all.

It's interesting, and often humorous, to look back at childhood as an adult. We understand so much more. When I look back at my youth, I have no idea how my mother had the energy to do everything she did, working full time and raising four children. We didn't have a lot of money, and yet I never felt as though we lacked anything. She may not have been able to buy us the latest toys or clothes, but she gave us more support, encouragement, and love than I could have thought possible. The youngest of four children, I was four years old when my parents divorced and my mom went to work full time to support us. This meant working all day as the secretary at our grade school, an exhausting job itself, and then working another full time job as our mother. She managed to make it to every sporting or extra-curricular event we participated in, read to us, played games with us, and did countless other things that made me think, as a little girl, that she could do anything. She somehow found time every night to spend quality time with us and it was the quality of this time together that I remember most.

As a little girl, my favorite time spent with my mother was bedtime. While our house was at times chaotic, with four very outgoing and loud kids running around, I recall my mother tucking me in as a very special time. Every night I had this time with her, just my mom and me, to talk about whatever I wanted. I valued this alone time incredibly and she never failed to stop whatever she was doing to spend it with me and tuck me in. There was something so special about lying in the dark, just before sleep, the house finally quiet, with my mom next to me to talk about anything I wanted. Sometimes I would vent about something my brother did that made me mad or tell her about something I did that day that I was proud of. Other times, she just rubbed my back and told me she loved me as I drifted off to sleep. Whatever mood the day had put me in, whether angry, anxious, excited, or happy, her familiar voice and presence next to me as I fell asleep always made every worry I had disappear. Sometimes I wish I could still call her right before I go to sleep to hear the words that she said every night when she left the room… "I love you, Kathy Jane."

Although my mom stopped tucking me in as I grew older (when it suddenly became "uncool"), her support and love were evident to me in so many other ways. Whether I was having a good day or the worst day ever, I knew I could talk with her and have that same feeling of support and peace that came over me every night when she tucked me in. In my adult life thus far, one of the biggest challenges for me was confronting my sexual orientation. For years I struggled with societal pressure to fit within the norm, always thinking that it wasn't me. However much I struggled with the pressures of society, I never once felt pressure from my mother. On the contrary, she made it clear from a very young age that she would love me for who I was, no matter what that ended up being. In junior high she began telling us that she would love us the same whether we were gay or straight. I don't think I understood the significance of that at the time, but as I was coming to terms with my own sexuality, I absolutely knew that my mom would support me and love me as much as she always had. She not only expressed this in words, but also showed it her actions. She respected all people and treated them equally regardless of gender, race, social class, religion, ability or sexual orientation. Racism, sexism, classism, heterosexism, or any other form of oppression, was not tolerated in our house. Growing up in a relatively small, homogenous town in the Midwest, my mother's ideals were incredibly progressive.

When I finally came out to my mom as a lesbian, her love and support were amazing. She told me that she loved me and was proud of me for being who I am. Actually, I think she probably told me that over a thousand times and still does almost every time I talk to her. She told me that she admired my strength. In reality, it was her strength that showed me that being honest about who I am, even though not everyone would support me, was more important than fitting into society's norms of who I "should" be. She modeled behavior that showed us that the most important thing in life is to love ourselves and others for who we are and to reject other people's biases and prejudices. Being raised by a woman who never judges others, who believes in herself, and who always shows compassion to others has been the greatest gift any person could ever give me. I hope to pass on her gifts to my children, so that they might learn the lessons she has taught me.

I am grateful beyond words for everything my mom has given me, but most of all, for being who she is and teaching me to love everything that I am.

* * * * *

NICK *born 1978*

At this point in my life, being a parent seems like a daunting and overwhelming responsibility. It also seems like too many young couples in my generation are diving headfirst into parenthood without the knowledge or parental guidance that leads to good parenting. And knowing the rate of divorce and number of single parents these days, parenting becomes an even more overwhelming responsibility. My parents divorced when I was six years of age. Most people think that this would have a negative impact on my childhood. I know the result was just the opposite.

One of the biggest and most important lessons I took from my childhood is the value of continuous support and selflessness. My mom was and is the perfect example. I remember countless times when my mom put myself and my siblings first – wait, that was ALL the time! I remember my mom driving my siblings and me to our soccer games on Saturday mornings not too long after dawn. I remember her watching my football games on Friday and Saturday nights, sitting in the cold rain, cheering on her son's team. I remember her going to almost every sports event that I was involved in…which was almost every one! I remember her unconditional support all through my childhood which helped me achieve the success I had in school and in sports and that I now have in life.

Every decision my mom faced was made with us kids as the priority for that decision. She gave me support. She gave me encouragement. She gave me unconditional love. This made me the person I am today and I am so very thankful for it. As an adult I realize how much of the person that I am today is a direct result of the parenting that I received. I learned to share what I was blessed with. Sometimes it was much harder than I thought (what kid wants to share their toys with their little sister?). I learned that trust and respect are not given freely, but they must be earned. I learned that love and support instills self-confidence and leadership. I will take all these things that I learned from my mom and pass them on to my kids.

I will forever be grateful to my mom for always being there for me – it means more to me than she can possibly imagine.

* * * * *

KELLY *born 1972*

Roxie, my mom, told me a long time ago that she wanted to write a book and share her stories of parenthood – in particular, raising four kids as a single parent and encouraging other young parents out there that it *is* possible, even on the days when it feels impossible. I wasn't surprised that she wanted to help others and share herself with the parenting community, that sounded just like her. But I also sensed in her the trepidation that anyone would feel when speaking as an assumed "authority" on a subject... she even once said to me, in an extremely rare moment of insecurity, "Who am I to write this book?"

Her four children – Mike, Nick, Kathy and I – are here to tell you who this woman is. My mom is a pillar of strength. She never gave up. She may have felt like it – probably from our terrible twos through the teenage years! – but she never once gave up, not on herself, not on the four of us. My mom is a living example of the person I want to be. She acts on the things she believes in, rather than just talking about them. She always speaks up for herself. She believes in herself more than anything else. She is willing to help anyone at anytime and gives of herself, and her time, unconditionally to everyone around her. Even though there were always four of us, I never felt ignored, never felt like we were a burden, never felt like less than my mom's top priority. (Secretly, I think we all feel like her "favorite" – pretty smooth on her part, eh?)

My mom is completely honest. She believes that the truth is always the best path and that if you speak from your heart, you'll always know the right thing to say. She taught us this at an extremely young age, making it possible for a five year old to come forward and admit he is the one that broke the crystal. (It was Nick. Butterfingers.) Because "you can't get in trouble if you tell the truth."

My mom is incredibly compassionate. She is truly accepting of all people and has taught us to never judge, never condemn a person for who they are. She has such a big heart and has passed on that open-minded attitude to her children. I think this is one of the most amazing traits to teach your kids – if all parents did this, imagine how the world could change.

My mom is not afraid to make mistakes – and admit to them. I'm sure you'll find this to be true as you read the book. She has always taught me that it's okay to fail and to be honest about making mistakes. She also taught me to forgive myself, learn from my mistakes, and move on. This lesson has helped me in my career every single step of the way.

My mom does everything with a sense of humor. Even on the toughest of days, she can find something to laugh about. She taught us the ability to laugh at ourselves and that laughter is a great cure for a bad mood. To this day, she can make even the most mundane chore fun and cheer me up with a few good laughs.

My mom raised us to be friends. If I absolutely had to choose one thing she passed on to me as my most treasured, it would be that she set the example of how to truly, unconditionally love one another. And that is what has led the four of us kids to be best friends, with her and with each other. She always treated us with fairness, with honesty, with total commitment, with respect, and with unending love. Those traits became the stage for how we treated each other. There were certainly many times of turmoil with four outgoing, outspoken kids growing up in the same house. My mom somehow managed to not only raise us with absolute grace, but raise us to be the most closely bonded family I know. Today, my siblings are my closest confidants, my support system, my sounding board, my absolute favorite people to be around. I can honestly say, I don't know anyone that feels the same as I do about their siblings. What an amazing gift.

I cannot even count the number of times people have said to me, "Wow, you have the greatest mom." Every time I hear it, I nod in excitement and say, "I know, I'm so lucky!" - but what I'm really thinking is *you don't even know the half of it*. Honestly, what could be better – and more valuable – in this life than having the world's greatest mom? (Someone should put that on a mug.) I hope that this book will serve the parenting community just as she hopes: that somewhere, someone will benefit from her story and be inspired to be the best parent they can be. As for this foreword, I hope it's a tiny reflection of how truly blessed and grateful I am that I somehow wound up with the most incredible person in the world to raise me, to guide me through childhood and adolescence, to teach me all the things I now love about myself, to be my role model in life, to be my biggest fan, to be my dearest friend.

* * * *

Mom, we are so grateful for the many gifts you have given us – most of all, for the person that you are every single day. We are so proud of you for sharing your story, as we know it will help countless parents (and therefore countless kids!).

We love you so very much. –Mike, Kathy, Nick & Kelly

INTRODUCTION

This is the book I needed to read when I became a single parent.

Scared to death and not knowing which way to turn during my divorce, I began to search my local library for books written by other single moms with four children. Not finding what I needed made me question myself all the more. Could I really do this?

My sense of humor became my guide to help me survive this new life with my children. They taught me so much more than I would have learned on my own. When I had fun, they had fun. Learning to focus on the positive things that happened during the day, instead of dwelling on the mistakes I made, helped to keep us all moving forward.

In writing this book, the individual stories describe what worked for me and what tools were needed to get me back in the game of life when all else failed. Learning to trust myself helped me start my life over. I desperately wanted my children to listen to me. What I learned is if I listened to them and incorporated their ideas into the solution, they felt part of the team. My hope is that this book will help you listen to yourself and each family member.

I wish to thank the following friends who were my readers and great support system: Mary Kay Smith, Gabriele Ertmann, Dr. Jane Lande, Kathy Fitzpatrick, Bev Greene, Barbara McFarland and Leslie Schubert. Your suggestions and kind words continued to carry me forward.

To my son, Mike, and friends, Barbara Bennett, Caroline Sheffield, Ginny Hanson and Patti Janes, who all went page by page with me, thank you for your devotion to my story in helping me to share it with others.

To my daughter, Kelly, your honesty, wisdom and laughter helped me through the tough times, keeping me motivated and inspired to continue writing while you were editing all the changes. Thank you for your unconditional love and support. You always made time for me, keeping me grounded and focused. You rock.

To Ben Skoda and Malcolm McIntyre, thank you for your final editing reviews and your professional guidance.

My love and deepest gratitude go to my four children, Kelly, Mike, Nick and Kathy Jane, who continued to challenge me to become a better me throughout our growing up years. You are my very favorite people in the whole wide world. Everyday you continue to inspire me. Your gifts of love and laughter will be puzzle pieces in my heart forever.

Chapter 1: Stupid Curfew

It was 3:15 a.m. and Nick, my 17-year-old son, still wasn't home. We had an argument earlier in the evening. I was the mean mom. He was the rebellious son. We had practiced this scene many times over in the past several months. Only this time, he pushed the curfew limit over the top.

The argument was about ... something. Honestly, I can't remember, but it must have seemed important at the time. His regular curfew was around 12:30 – 1 a.m., with the understanding that if he was going to be late, he would call me. 1:30 came and no phone call. I considered that he was showing his independence and his desire not to have any curfew at all. He reminded me many times that none of his friends had a stupid curfew. Inside, the knot in my stomach ached. Anger overwhelmed me, as I grew tired and just a little worried.

My youngest daughter, Kathy, who was 15, had already come home after spending the evening with friends. She knew my worried look and didn't want me to wait alone. As we were chatting, we flipped the TV channel to a movie and began watching it together. After the movie ended, I suggested that she go to bed and I would wake her when Nick got home. She decided to stay up and we continued to search for another late night movie. Secretly, I was relieved to have her company. Just her presence helped keep my anger in check and my mind from being tormented with worry.

2:30 a.m. and still no sign of Nick. Worry now replaced the anger. I had no one to call. I couldn't begin calling his friends' parents to see if he was with any of them because I didn't know which of his friends he ended up with that particular evening. The thought of a car accident plagued my mind. Calling the emergency rooms of the local hospitals, ER nurses from both hospitals told me that no teenagers were in their care presently. *What does that mean? Had he been there earlier and just released? Was he still in a ditch somewhere?* I tried to remain calm. Worry and anger fought for my attention. Worry prevailed.

As soon as his headlights flashed in our driveway, Kathy headed upstairs to her bedroom. She turned and said, "I'll always call."

"Thanks."

My gut told me not to show my anger, as I would have pushed him further away. Now that I knew he was safe, I wanted to scream and shout at him. Surely that had worked for me in the past. How inconsiderate he had been. Deep breaths. More deep breaths. Then, in a calm voice that even I didn't recognize, the following words came out of my mouth as he entered our home, "I'm glad you're safe. I'm too angry to discuss this right now but we'll talk first thing tomorrow morning because I don't deserve to spend the night this worried."

Silently, we both went to our rooms.

****

Learning that a cooling off time was good for everyone, we were able to discuss the issues more calmly and find a workable solution. This came with years of practice.

Chapter 2: The Early Years

In a compulsive quest to please others, we can abandon
who we are, losing a sense of self, a sense of identity.
Lee Jampolsky. Ph D

Within the first six months of my marriage, a gnawing feeling in the pit of my stomach told me that something wasn't quite right. I just didn't know what that something was. I thought I was living my dream: being married, wanting children and beginning the rest of our lives together. Ignoring the uneasy feeling in my gut, I pushed ahead. Through the years, my dream of "they all lived happily ever after" was shattered by divorce. Instead, my story became one of being a divorced mother with four young children and our uphill climb for survival over a period of 20-plus years. My children were young when the divorce occurred. Kathy was 4, Nick was 6, Mike was 8 and Kelly was 11.

The divorce felt like a ton of bricks had been dumped on us. When I moved one brick, two more took its place. Slowly, very slowly, we began to sort through the rubble.

Over the years, our divorced family gradually grew into a larger family. Today we spend holidays together – I'm talking about the divorced parents, my former husband, Jerry, his wife, Jean and their three children, April, Jake and Cole, myself and our children, Kelly, Mike, Nick and Kathy. Celebrating holidays together with Jerry and his family could not have occurred at the beginning of the divorce, but over time, we remembered we created our children in love and we continue to join together with them throughout the years. Never was this part of my earlier plan, nor would it have been feasible immediately after our divorce. However, over time and putting the children's needs and interests as a priority, our holidays became a wonderful time of unity shared by all. My story is how we arrived in the togetherness.

I spent my childhood doing what I was told and never talking back to my parents. I didn't have a voice. Maybe all kids didn't during the 50s and 60s. Harriet B. Braiker states in her book, *The Disease to Please,* "If children are taught by parents to be pleasers, when those children reach adolescence, they will begin to please their peers instead of making decisions to satisfy their own internal needs."

Trying to please others helped me to realize that I wanted to make it different for my kids. My commitment to myself was to change from being a people pleaser and learn to speak out for myself. That should be easy enough, right? And then, I would teach my children to speak out for their needs. I didn't think it would be that hard. Little did I know what was ahead.

Growing up, my dad was gruff and straight to the point. He still is. I realize now that part of me was a little afraid of him – or maybe I was just more afraid to disappoint him. But I always knew exactly what to do (and for me, that was whatever he said).

My mom always reminded me that what others thought about my behavior was more important than what I thought, especially if I did something wrong. Shame and guilt were constant reminders during my childhood years. I'm sure she was taught that from her parents and just passed it on to me.

Over the years, I have learned to appreciate that my parents did the very best they could and I love them for that. I admire the accomplishments they have achieved in their lifetime. My survival mode became a strong work ethic taught to me by my parents. I'll always be grateful to them for modeling that behavior.

****

My divorce made me question my past and the choices that I am responsible for. What changes do I need to make going forward? Change can be difficult.

Chapter 3: The Beginning

Society's message to women during my high school years in the 60s was to choose a career as a teacher, secretary or a nurse. The underlying message was for girls to find a husband, stay home and raise a family. College or joining the workforce was seen as the avenue to meet a future husband.

I met my future husband, Jerry, while attending Iowa State University in Ames, Iowa. (Right on track here with society's standard.) He was in the college of engineering and I was studying to be an elementary education teacher. Several years after college, Jerry and I were married and two years later, we began our family. Over the next 14 years of marriage and four children later, we had grown further and further apart. We tried counseling but nothing helped us back to a combined journey.

It was the fall of 1984, and I was in the middle of a divorce with four children, ages four, six, eight and eleven. I was scared to death. During our marriage, Jerry and I had agreed that I would stay home with our children and he would work outside of the home. Being a stay-at-home mom made me feel grateful to have the opportunity to spend the time with them, guiding and shaping their lives (which is what I thought I was doing).

While I was trying to guide our kids, they became a powerful force in my life. They began to mold, change and create new patterns in my life as well. Because they continued to challenge me every single day, I had to constantly choose to listen, learn and grow in order to keep my head above water and manage some semblance of control.

Many times I felt submerged underwater and would come to the surface gasping for breath, feeling the weight of four young children resting on my shoulders, knowing at any minute, we might go back under. Many times we did. It was that pressure which caused me to focus on helping myself while helping them. In essence, my children and I were guiding each other. We became a team. They constantly pushed me to a higher level, and I had to work on my thought processes and beliefs to continually challenge my inner self to become stronger, more outspoken and definitely more driven than I had ever been.

The feelings we develop about our life and ourselves, from birth through childhood, are formative for us as we enter adulthood. In childhood, we have an opportunity to develop a sense of trust, not only in others, but in ourselves as well. Growing up, I knew I hadn't learned to fully believe in myself and my decisions. Instead, I had learned to please others. Now going through a divorce, I began to question myself over and over... *Could I do this parenting job alone?* Looking back, I know it was something I learned to do with the help of my children. It was also this trust that I desperately wanted to create in my own children – to believe in themselves and have the ability to know how and when to believe in others. The way I had it pictured in my head was: *Trust = to believe and rely on my own judgments + strength = self confidence.*

Can I re-learn this myself and then teach it to my children? How?

The divorce had stripped away any remnants of trust, self-confidence and self-esteem that I once had. My work began.

My mind raced. *When my daughter is 15 and dating, will she be strong enough to be in touch with her feelings and do what is right for her and make her own decisions or will she give in to peer pressure and try to please her boyfriend? When my son is 16 and driving with his friends in the car, will he be strong enough to say 'no' to drinking and driving, or will he surrender to peer pressure? How do I teach my children to think for themselves and speak their mind?*

Other questions continued to swirl in my head. *What qualities do I want my children to possess when they are age 25? How do I start teaching those qualities while they are young? What do I expect from my children and how do I create that environment in my home?*

If someone could have just told me how to do all this by myself, and correctly, of course, that would have made it easier for me. Only then would I have felt good about what I had accomplished. I was a long way from that dream.

In our divorce, the judge awarded Jerry and me joint custody; however, I was given physical custody so the children were with me all of the time except for every other weekend. It was one of the most frightening times of my life. Even people from my church told me to "patch things up" with my husband, because I would never make it on my own, financially, emotionally or physically. Guess what? They were wrong; however, even I didn't know that at the time.

At first I delved into this single parenting situation and truly wanted to succeed because I felt my children deserved it. They were amazing children (and what children aren't?). Feeling that they didn't deserve the divorce of their parents, I was going to make that up to them by being the very best mom I could be. My children became my motivation for me to do a good job as a single parent.

In the mornings, I was up and going with my hair on fire before the kids were even out of bed. I had showered, dressed, and started the second load of laundry with breakfast on the table when they finally woke up. I wanted so much for them to think that nothing was going to change with their father gone. I wanted to do it all.

That didn't last. Being physically and emotionally exhausted, I had nothing left to give. Failure set in.

Doubt and fear became my constant companions. The fight of my life began. Doubt told me I couldn't be a single parent because so many people kept telling me I couldn't do it alone. Previously, when I was still married, I felt I was doing a good job as a stay-at-home mom and certainly had my hands full with all the activities of the children with two adults in the home. Now I was taking on the impossible.

Fear was the nagging voice in my head with his message of failure, *You can't do this. Who do you think you are? Everyone is telling you that you can't do it, why can't you listen to them?* Every day I questioned myself. I'd never felt so isolated in all my life, and yet I was surrounded by these four precious faces.

I felt desperate. As a last resort one night as I was crying myself to sleep again, I looked inside my heart and knew I had to just believe in myself and continue to walk forward all alone. It was very scary for me. Just trust myself. That became my nightly prayer.

What kept me going forward was my belief that my children deserved a better life. I vowed to myself I would do my best to make sure their needs were met and to help them grow in an atmosphere of love and understanding.

Doubt and fear continued. *How can I do that since I had just failed at my marriage with one other person...how can I succeed with four people?*

This was the beginning of learning that the motivation had to come from within me because it was my intention for myself to be a good parent, not for anyone else. The children would just happen to be the recipients.

By being intentional about learning to be the best parent I could be, first, I had to acknowledge that I was choosing to give something that I wouldn't know if I was successful until many years later. Knowing that, I still chose to care for the human spirit with love, understanding, sharing and genuine respect for myself and my children. There would be no immediate feedback. No one was there to encourage me along the way... no one would be there to say, "Thanks. You're doing a good job." All of that feedback had to come from within me.

****

Fear continued his dance with me on many nights. For a long time, I wore him like a second skin. It certainly wasn't easy, but remembering my intention about learning to be the best parent I could be, brought me back to allow love and listening in my heart (again and again and again).

Chapter 4: Pulling Up the Bootstraps

Financial stability became another one of my motivational forces. Applying for a position at the children's school, a K-8 building, allowed me to have the same hours as they had and some time off in the summer to spend with them. Landing the job became a lifesaver. Not that the job was easy, but it gave me the opportunity to see my children all day long in the halls and get to know their friends and teachers.

I witnessed a lot. At times, I observed parents yelling at their kids right in front of everyone. Now I know what that looked like for both the parent and the child. My heart always went to the child. Part of me felt sorry for the parents because they were so out of control. *Is that what I looked like to my children at times? What will they remember about me?* I took it all in and replayed many of the scenes in my head, trying to learn from them all.

Then one day, I saw a loving mom who came to pick up her sixth grade son who had accidentally wet his pants in class. The love in her eyes and her warm, inviting smile greeted her son as she put her arm around him and assured him that this happens to all of us. Immediately, I saw the relief in his face. As she was guiding him out the door, I heard her say to him in a soothing voice that they would go home and clean up and enjoy lunch together. Then she would bring him back to class. I remember thinking, *I want to show my children that kind of love.*

That day I loved my job.

Another motivational force was created as I promised myself that I would treat my children as I wanted to be treated. Making sure their voices were heard and validated was important to me. At the top of my list was making each of them feel loved and heard.

At this same time, I was also trying to read everything I could get my hands on about single parenting and what to expect from children being raised in a single parent home. It wasn't easy finding time to read. Actually nothing was easy during this time period.

Reading for me came either late at night or early morning as they were all tucked in their cozy little beds and every other weekend when they were with their dad. In all of the books, the recurring theme was to take care of yourself first and then care for those around you.

That message, I was sure, was meant for everyone else because I had four children and knew I didn't have time for me. Paying attention to how to care for the kids and what was best for them became my focus. Worrying about how they were surviving and how the divorce would affect them caused me not to sleep very well.

I was struggling.

****

Our bodies teach us about ourselves when something is not right. All we have to do is pay attention.

Chapter 5: The Breakdown

Feeling like I was going crazy —with friends telling me I couldn't do this by myself —brought feelings of loneliness and a fear of failure. Checking out a library book called *Crazy Time: Surviving Divorce*, by Abigail Trafford and just skimming parts of it seemed to help. But mostly, I remember just seeing the name of the book on my bedside table. It made me feel like there were others experiencing the same feeling so much that a book was written with that exact title. For some reason, it told me that what I was feeling was normal.

I just wanted to feel normal.

My divorce and the time leading up to it had thrown me into such a deep depression that I felt like I was just going through the motions of living. I had lost a lot of weight and looked unhealthy. My face was so thin and gaunt, I actually looked malnourished. In a short period of time, my hair began to fall out and I developed gum disease from all the stress. I was trying so hard to prove to the children (and myself) that nothing had changed and that I could do everything by myself, that we would make it. My energy was depleted. Nothing was working.

I hit rock bottom while sitting in the oral surgeon's chair having gum surgery. I literally cried non-stop for over an hour and a half in the chair. Meanwhile the surgeon stopped repeatedly, asking me if I was in pain. Assuring him I didn't feel anything that was going on in my mouth, I continually promised he wasn't hurting me.

What was hurting was the fact that my body was giving me the signs that what I was doing wasn't working. I felt like I was falling apart.

Actually, I was falling apart. I didn't know how to fix everything that was broken. Now add to that, embarrassment and humiliation that I was having this crying episode in front of the entire oral surgery team. Fear set in. *How do I keep going? What do I do next?*

Having breakfast with my friend, Ginny, and telling her about my embarrassing breakdown in the dentist's chair, validated to me that I was going down the tubes. Still, I repeatedly told her that I was going to make it because the kids were worth it. At the end of our conversation, Ginny said she had heard me say three times during breakfast that the kids were worth it but she hadn't heard me say that I was worth it.

Her statement took my breath away. I quickly assured her, of course, I was worth it, but during the drive home that same day, the tears came pouring down my cheeks again. I realized I wasn't really sure how I felt. I had to figure it out: Am I worth it?

My next thought was, *my kids deserve better than this; I'm not even fun to be around anymore.* I had always prided myself on my quick wit and my ability to make people laugh which has begun many a friendship for me and is a great way to entertain myself. However, somewhere along the line, I had set aside my sense of humor and even I wasn't enjoying being around myself these days.

What was actually happening was that I was going through the normal grieving process. I was grieving the loss of my marriage, the loss of my dream of living as a family together for the rest of our lives, and the loss of my married life, emotionally, physically, financially and socially. Deciding then to make a plan of action, I wasn't going to allow my grieving to completely shut me down. While giving myself permission to grieve, I also decided to get back into the game. Having a plan made me feel more in control.

My plan was twofold: to take a parenting class to try to find new ways of managing my whole new life, and secondly, to answer the ultimate question: Am I worth it?

****

During these difficult times, I struggled to embrace the darkness. Learning that discomfort inspired change, I knew I had to find the power within me to move forward

Chapter 6: Am I Worth It?

The paradox of change is that we can't affect deep change
until we first accept ourselves just as we are.
Lee Jampolsky, Ph.D.

Along with my parenting classes, I scheduled counseling appointments to answer the question once and for all: Am I Worth It? Identifying my own self-worth was important because I had to figure out if I was strong enough to mentor my children in the days ahead.

Self-worth and parenting go hand-in-hand.

Webster's dictionary defined worth as the quality within a person that renders him deserving of respect. Since divorce had thrown the scarlet letter around my neck, I was very conscious of society's message of failure that I was wearing. Could I break through that failure facade and begin to respect myself so that I could tackle the most important role of parenting that was before me? It wouldn't make any difference how many parenting classes I had taken; if I didn't respect myself, I wouldn't be able to implement the techniques. I felt like I was on shaky ground and thought counseling could help.

The importance of selecting the right counselor was a lesson I learned by trial and error. Wearing my "naive hat," I thought all counselors were the same. Learning that the first or second session should have given me an indication of compatibility for my particular needs was an important lesson. Looking at the situation as an interview for both client and counselor to learn what the problem areas are and how they will be addressed is how I have approached counseling since then. They don't have the answers but it's their job to ask the right questions to help me find the answers from within myself.

After staying in sessions with one counselor for about three months and not feeling any connection with him, I finally realized that I wasn't making any progress. Out of frustration, I took a risk and searched for a new counselor to start over again. A nice surprise. After the very first session with my new counselor, and feeling heard right from the beginning, it was an easy transition to fill in the rest of my story. The new therapist validated my feelings and gave me suggestions of how to begin making changes from that first session on. She asked me some questions and I came up with the plan that resonated with my inner feelings.

Making the change in counselors was an "ah-ha" moment for me: I was trusting my gut feeling. Previously, my gut was telling me the other counselors weren't hearing me. I just wasn't listening to my inner voice. It felt good to know I had the answer all along, just frustrating that I waited so long before making the change.

My new therapist focused right from the beginning on my statement of why I began counseling: Am I worth It? She asked me to remember back to my childhood and whether I valued my opinion or someone else's. It was as easy as that. Because I was raised to value other people's opinions more than my own, I knew where to begin my work. My mother role-modeled that behavior because that is what was taught to her. It was typical of her generation, who believed we need to please other people more than ourselves. No blame is assigned here; just the insight that my parents, doing the best they could, passed on to me what they were taught and the rest was my job to make some changes.

Doubt quickly stepped forward asking, *How can I give to my kids something that I didn't receive from my parents?*

With the knowledge that I was looking to other people for approval, I knew I needed to look within myself and decide if I liked me for who I am. Sounds easy enough, but when I began to face these questions, I wasn't sure how to actually do the work.

My counselor suggested I list all of the things that I liked about myself on a sheet of paper. Doubt began jumping up and down in my head with tons of negative messages about me. This was going to be more difficult than I had imagined. Trying to muster up something positive, this is what I wrote the first time:

Things I Like About Me:

1. Sense of Humor
2. Humor – sense of
3. Of humor – sensing it will pull me out of this hellhole I am in
4. The End

Sad little story, isn't it? That's how I felt as I began to explore the things I liked about me. It was difficult for me to try to put other qualities on paper because I felt like I was bragging or thought I was better than someone else. That's how insecure I felt at the time. My self-esteem must have registered about a -12. If I did have one good thought about myself, doubt quickly took its place.

Then my counselor helped me cross another barrier. She asked me to sit quietly by myself (she apparently had forgotten about the four little darlings at home because "quietly" never existed at our house). Nevertheless, my assignment was to imagine sitting across from myself like a friend would and write the qualities that I saw in me, as a friend. This was her way of describing how I can step outside of myself and try to look at myself more objectively.

I can still remember doing this exercise. Looking at myself, I thought: *Well, hi there, foxy Roxie. You're looking mighty cute in that hot pink sweat suit that you've worn for the past four days. Wait, what's that smell? Did you slather on some "pew-fume"? Mmmmmm, smells nice.*

I tried to focus on myself as my friend. Trust me, this was difficult to do. Slowly, the list began:

1. Sense of Humor (even if I'm the only one who understands it)
2. Trustworthy
3. Honest
4. Strong work ethic

5. Giving
6. Caring
7. Loving
8. Loyal
9. Able to bark on command & doesn't shed (much)
10. Treats others like I would like to be treated

Once I read the list, I was a little surprised. I knew I wasn't perfect. I certainly made mistakes, but I can honestly say I felt I had those qualities most of the time.

The next step: If I really believed I possessed those qualities, why was I giving my power over to believing some negative messages in my head that someone else had said about me?

That's it. I was giving my power away to someone else. Over time, their messages became more important and stronger than my own feelings about myself. My job at hand was to take my power back.

At first, becoming angry at the people who said the negative things about me consumed my thoughts. My counselor suggested another tactic. I could continue expending the energy I was using to fuel the anger I was feeling towards others. Or use that energy to motivate myself to get those negative messages out of my head, replacing them with my own personal messages about myself. Interesting choice. Making the decision to use the energy to motivate myself with my own personal messages moved me forward.

Once I was able to step back from the anger, I could understand that my anger didn't change or have any effect on the people I was angry with. Their lives continued just the same as before. The only person I can change is myself. I was the one who had allowed those negative messages to stay in my head and it was my responsibility to clear them out. For a while, I spent my time being angry with myself for allowing someone else's messages to stay in my head and was doing a very good job of beating myself up for letting it happen for such a long time. If only there was an award for Best Beater-Upper of Self, I definitely would have received that trophy. My counselor brought me back to doing the work on myself.

One of the suggestions in counseling was to think of the negative messages as a video tape. My job was to push the eject button once I started hearing the negative messages and replace the negative tape with a brand new one that only I could record messages on. *What do I truly believe about me?* The answer to that question needed to be on my video tape in my head... my own version of me. *Will it work?*

The counselor helped me by suggesting each week I use a Post-it note on my bathroom mirror of what quality I wanted to focus on that day. By narrowing my attention to one positive quality about myself each day, I began to gradually take my power back. Then when the negative messages came roaring into my brain, I would push the eject button and insert my own blank tape.

Notching it up a bit, I identified the negative message as a troll message. Then, in my mind I would get my megaphone out and a mini me dressed in a cheerleading outfit would yell, "Eject! Eject!" My own positive words about myself were then put on the blank tape in my head.

Crazy as it was, it worked. That cheerleader was definitely overworked but she got the job done.

Doubt had a heyday with this procedure as I was learning it which I expressed to my counselor, "You mean to tell me, that writing one word on a puny, sticky note on my bathroom mirror is going to help make me feel better about myself?"

There, I guess I told her.

The counselor stated that anything you repeat 21 days in a row becomes a habit. *There, I guess she told me.*

Lucky me, I just happened to have a lot of "21 days in a row" ahead of me.

And then I remembered: *What I put into this is what I will receive back.* I needed to be at the top of my game, feeling good about me in every sense so that I would feel love for myself in order to give the same to my children. Every three weeks, the puny, one-word note on my bathroom mirror would change to a new reminder of a quality that I wanted to embrace and record on my video tape in my head.

I can still remember the first day I started the puny note on the bathroom mirror routine. The word I chose was humor. That's what I kept repeating in my head: *I have a good sense of humor.*

On my way to work, I thought, *Wouldn't it be funny if each of us told everyone who asked, exactly how we felt that day? For example: I imagined co-workers saying, "Good morning, how are you?"*

Instead of my usual, "Fine, and you?" Wouldn't they be totally shocked and surprised if I answered with, "Actually, I am going through a divorce right now and have absolutely no self-esteem. If you have a little bit of self-esteem left over this morning, could I just borrow some for today? Because I have nothing, zero, zip, nada."

I imagined a surprised, shocked look on their faces as they slowly and quietly backed away.

And that's how I started my day for the next 21 days. When a co-worker asked, "How are you?," a huge smile crossed my lips and out of my mouth, I managed to say, "Fine, and you?" but in my mind, I was imagining the shocked look I really wanted to see on their faces if I had answered differently. It actually felt good to laugh just with myself about the little game I was creating to entertain just me.

It meant I was getting back in the game.

The "Am I Worth It?" work continued on, with many sticky notes of one word messages for me to have fun with over the next several months. Even today, I remain committed to the positive video messages in my head. When I experience a setback, I take any negative words out that may have recorded over time and put my own blank tape inside my head and record a positive message "to me – from me".

This also helps me to revisit the patterns that I have established in my life and to make changes when something isn't working for me. The image I create as my intention helps manifest that outcome in each day going forward.

For me, counseling became an act of courage. Looking at who I really was through my own eyes, and then making choices of where I wanted to be and how I could work to get there kept me listening to my inner voice. Anger motivated me to make positive changes in my life. I can't control other people's thoughts or actions but I can control my own. Other people's words and behavior are about them. My actions and my words are about me.

And the good news I learned: I'm worth it.

****

Counseling is an act of courage. We learn who we are by finding the answers within ourselves and stating them out loud.

Chapter 7: The Parenting Class

Children are not a distraction from more important work.
They are the most important work. C. S. Lewis

Even just signing up for parenting classes helped me feel like I was making some sort of progress. (Parent Academy, ready or not, here I come.) Any forward motion felt good at this point. If I picked up one valuable idea from the class, then I knew I was on the right path. Actually, the truth is, I also just wanted to go out for pie and coffee with my friend, Ginny and talk (i.e., whine) about how hard parenting is and compare notes. I wanted ideas from her about what was working at her house with her four children.

Once, we were talking on the phone and it seemed unusually quiet at her house. Inquiring about what she had done with her two little ones, I wanted to find out why she seemed to be very relaxed and enjoying our free time to chat. In comparison, I felt like I was dancing a jig to pull out toys and cheerios to entertain my kids. She said she had given them a jello mold and they were having fun.

I said, "A jello mold? How is that entertaining them?"

Ginny said, "They love squishing it through their fingers."

Gasping, I eeked out, "You mean it had jello in it?"

She laughed and said, "Sometimes you just have to do what it takes to get the job done." We both roared in laughter. I will never forget that.

Some days, "craziness" was normal.

Then, another awakening. The series of parenting classes would begin changes in me that would affect the rest of my life.

There were 35 to 40 adults in the room, and the instructor walked to the head of the class and gave a brief outline of that evening's discussion. I was starting to feel better, back in control. *Baby steps, baby steps.*

The instructor began that first night by asking us to write our goals for parenting our children. Anxiety set in. *Goals? Is she kidding? Now we need goals? Maybe I'm in the wrong class.*

She had to be kidding. *The goal was that parents would feed, clothe and send their children to school and the kids would grow up and at age 18, they would move out of the house. Isn't that the goal?*

Previously, I had never thought about individual goals for parenting. So as I looked around the room and saw people actually writing things down, I thought that I should at least make a grocery list or something and make it look like I was writing down goals. I had no idea what to write.

Who are these people? And how can they have goals already? And what kind of pie do I really want after this class is over?

The familiar concept that my parents drilled into my head came front and center: *If you're going to do something, take the time to do it right.* That was quickly followed by: *Whatever you put into something is what you receive back.*

Feeling pressured, I wrote:

1. To have fun every day (yeah, like that would happen)
2. To survive (smiling while writing this one)
3. To let the children survive (smiling even more now)

My thoughts were interrupted when the presenter told us in a few minutes we would be discussing our goals, so I quickly wrote something in case we had to present one of our goals out loud. I wanted to make sure that I had something everyone else would think was extremely intelligent (that's how people pleasers think). So I quickly wrote:

4. To grow together.

(Not really knowing what that exactly meant but envisioning all the children and myself literally growing together where our skin was actually attached and trying to walk somewhere as a group. Knowing how difficult it is to walk in a three-legged race, I was picturing all five of us trying to hustle through the grocery store as this loud, ten-legged amoeba.)

For years afterwards, I have often thought of those goals and how often the number one goal came into play for me: to have fun everyday.

Mornings were the hardest, except for after school, dinner time and getting ready for bed... and any other time they were awake. Quite often at 6:30 a.m. when the kids were fighting about some mundane issue while getting ready for school, I would ask myself, *And what part of this is fun for me? Don't you remember my prayer last night was begging for more patience? Did you think I meant patients?* While headed in the direction of the noise, I reminded myself to take some deep breaths and then some more.

Reaching the scene of the crime, I began singing a song with a pretend microphone, and after a few lines, I would pass the pretend microphone to them and they would join in. Their imagination was far superior to mine so they loved joining in the game.

Changing the subject and getting their attention were definitely ways to distract them from fighting about mundane issues and helped to get them back on track. It was fun for both them and me. That was when they were very young, but it proved the point effective when, instead of focusing on their fighting, if I began having fun myself, they would join in.

My inner child was alive and engaged in the fun.

As they grew older (about second grade), each of them picked out their own alarm clock and learned how to set the alarm so they could begin their morning and learn to accept responsibility for being on time for school. It only took them one tardy at school to learn they didn't like the consequences of their own actions of being late. Those consequences came from the teacher, which took the "bad guy" label away from me - as I seemed to wear that cloak way too often as it was.

That, of course, all sounds very adult. Like I thought of it because I was bored one day and said, *How can I nurture Kelly's self esteem and confidence by getting to school on time? Why don't we go out together and pick out an alarm clock?*

Nope, it happened because I yelled at her in the morning to quit "dawdling." I'm not even sure if she knew what that meant, and continued to yell at her to "hurry up and eat her breakfast and stop playing with the other kids – stop dawdling."

Her crime: she took her time getting dressed and actually talked and laughed with her brothers and sister at the breakfast table. How horrible.

This particular morning and yes, I still remember it, she left for school crying while I was still yelling at her to hurry up so she wouldn't be late. It was only two seconds after she had left that I began crying. *How could I have sent my daughter to school crying? Why do I keep yelling at her every morning?*

Those statements continued to torment me all day. Her breakfast was probably churning in her stomach as she was running the two blocks to school. What a terrible way for her to start her day and the only thing she was guilty of was engaging in conversation with her siblings. I definitely needed to change our morning routine.

None of this was fun.

All day long I kept thinking about what I would say to her after school. Finally, I came up with the plan. Begin with the truth. First I would apologize for my behavior and tell her how sorry I was that I had yelled so much that she left for school crying.

No excuses from me about how slow she moved in the morning and that it drove me CRAZY that she took too much time eating breakfast. None of that or it would just negate the apology. First, just the apology and owning my behavior that I was in the wrong.

This was hard for me. In my head, I wanted to explain that it was her fault for driving me crazy with her pokey little puppy routine every morning and playing with everyone. I had to concentrate on owning my behavior. (That lesson I had to learn over and over.)

Sharing with her that I didn't feel very good about myself when I was yelling at her to hurry in the mornings, made me feel vulnerable. Making the statement that she and I are both very smart girls, we should be able to come up with some ideas that would solve this problem. She liked being called smart. I definitely had her attention now.

Asking her what she thought might work was the next step. Not missing a beat, she suggested that she could pick out her school clothes that she was going to wear the night before, which might help. (Never mind that I had suggested this a gazillion times before and it never caught on.) However, I jumped at the opportunity to give her credit for a great idea.

We both high-fived each other.

Suggesting we go to the store where she could pick out an alarm clock that would wake her up every morning to music sealed the deal. Telling her she had earned the privilege of having her own alarm clock and the responsibility of getting dressed and coming downstairs when she was ready because she was getting so much older was just what she needed to hear. Kelly loved the idea. She was more than willing to accept more responsibility.

Suggesting that she could set the stove buzzer during breakfast, and it would let her know when it was ten minutes before she had to leave for school also worked for us. Kelly knew from other children who had been tardy to school that they had to stay inside at recess and make up that time. She never was late for school, however, she left several mornings without finishing her breakfast and told me how hungry she was before lunch.

It wasn't long before her breakfast was eaten completely before the buzzer went off. I repeatedly told her that she must be very proud of herself for accepting this responsibility to get ready for school all by herself.

In the meantime, I had to practically staple my mouth shut every morning just to let it unfold as it should.

Redirecting my children's behavior at times when they were misbehaving or fighting didn't happen overnight or come to me automatically. It was learned through trial and error. Starting with the quick fix methods, such as yelling at them to stop what they were doing, or when that didn't work, I cleverly went to yelling louder at them to stop what they were doing. Sometimes I resorted to solving the fights myself which, naturally, escalated to more fighting because the child who didn't get their way was now arguing with me that so-and-so had their turn first the last time and that it was their turn to be first today. With four kids, I couldn't remember who went first last time. Go figure.

It seemed like a never-ending battle. I always felt like the bad guy which led me (finally) to be more creative and ask the children how to solve the fight or bring them into the solution by changing their focus, which worked the majority of the time. By redirecting their behavior, I was able to stop most of the fighting. Asking each of them, how they would suggest we solve this problem and negotiating with them a solution that they all agreed with worked for us.

At times, I regressed and stepped in and solved the argument just because it was quicker (and it seemed I was always in a hurry). But, when I took the time to ask the kids how to resolve their own issues, the solutions seemed to last longer and everyone felt heard. Sometimes they would turn the situation into all of us laughing, such as one of the kids jokingly suggesting a good solution would be for them to "hog the toy the entire hour so no one else could play with it." When we were laughing and having a good time, we felt like a team again.

Sometimes they were the ones who showed me when it was time to teach them something new. Like the time when Kelly, age 7, and Mike, age 4, were invited over to our 80-year-old neighbor's home for milk and cookies. When they arrived back home a half hour later, I inquired if they had a good time.

Kelly said, "Yeah, we sure did. Mike was really good. He played with Mrs. H's underarm fat the whole time she played the piano for us."

It was then I knew that I should have the "don't-play-with-anyone's-underarm-fat-talk" with the kids.

When the children were young, they would come to me and tell me that they were bored because they didn't have anything to do. I quickly responded by asking them to clean out the silverware drawer or get out the vacuum and run it throughout the house. They would look shocked and tell me that they didn't want to do work, they wanted to play.

Our discussion then turned to how they were the only ones who knew what they really liked to do and felt like doing. If they came to me telling me they were bored, I couldn't make them happy. Only they can make themselves happy. We discussed that sometimes we just have to try several things before we find something we enjoy doing. I encouraged them to try finding what they enjoyed doing on their own.

We then made a pact: if they came to me and said they were bored, I could assign them a job and they would have to agree to do it because they were asking me to make them happy. Smart kids. They learned very quickly to entertain themselves.

As they grew older, by including their ideas into the solution, it usually seemed to have everyone's attention and cooperation and the problems were solved to their satisfaction. More baby steps.

My goal became: Have a good sense of humor – buy one, rent one, borrow one... I must have one. When I'm around someone who's having a good time, I can't help but join in.

It was the same for my kids.

****

Setting goals is important in whatever you're trying to accomplish and proved invaluable to me in my parenting. The goal I set to have fun everyday placed the responsibility right on my shoulders because I am the only person that can make me happy. Then my job was to teach each of my children that it was their responsibility to make themselves happy. When we look within ourselves for the answers, we are learning to be internally motivated and don't expect others to solve our problems.

Chapter 8: Children's Fears

One particular parenting class changed the rest of my life beginning that very night. The instructor began by stating that all of us have fears. She said we would go around the room and each name two of our own fears.

Immediately, panic set in. *What two fears could I possibly talk about that sound "adult"?* I certainly couldn't say I was deathly afraid of snakes and flying (which unfortunately, is the absolute truth). I had been told that those were stupid fears and I believed that (darn people pleaser thing again).

Suddenly, the instructor pointed to the man in the front row and asked him to start us off.

He began, "Well, I'm afraid of spiders and..."

I didn't hear the rest because as soon as he said "spiders," relief immediately settled throughout my body. His fears were just like mine. I knew it was safe to say, "snakes and the fear of flying." My body relaxed as we went around the room of adults admitting fears of being alone, the dark, public speaking, mice, heights, being out of control, strangers, storms, snakes, flying, guns, thunder, lightning, dogs, worms, birds, bats, scary movies, large crowds, hospitals, dentists, doctors, shots, elevators, bugs, etc. This was all from the adults in the room. It felt good to know there were others with similar fears.

Then the instructor looked at the gentleman in the front row and said, "How would you feel if I said, 'Don't be afraid of spiders. They won't hurt you. You're so much bigger than they are. They're really afraid of you so you don't need to be afraid of them'?"

He said, "That doesn't help me one bit; I'm still afraid."

She asked, "Did you feel heard?"

"No," he replied.

She said, "Would you want to discuss it with me again?"

"No," he replied.

She asked, "Why?" and he stated, "Because you don't understand. You're going to try and talk me out of it."

The instructor told us that's what we do to our children. When they tell us something, we deny their fear and say, "You're a big boy; you shouldn't be afraid."

Or "You don't want to be a cry baby all the time. That didn't even hurt when you fell. Be a big girl and stop crying."

Or "Other boys and girls aren't afraid of lightning, and you want to be a big boy too, right? Lighting is nothing to be afraid of."

Instead she asked the gentleman, "How would you feel if I said, 'Yeah, those spiders do look kind of creepy and they build those sticky webs and hang in the air and have those long legs and run everywhere'?"

He replied quickly, "Yeah, I'm right there with ya." The whole class laughed.

Her point was that he had been heard and his fear was validated. When someone is heard and validated, they begin to build a trust with you and tell you how they feel because you have created a safe place for them to express themselves.

This concept is critical because it affects every relationship we have. What I learned that night made so much sense to me: validate others' feelings and gain their trust. They know you are listening.

That night changed the way I have related to my children, my friends, my co-workers and everyone with whom I have a conversation. It felt good. It felt like common sense.

The instructor gave examples of talking with our children about working through their fears. Her example was children who are afraid of the dark. Tell them that you were afraid of the dark when you were little, and one of the things that helped you was to have a night-light in your room and then you could see if you got up to go to the bathroom. Or if you woke up in the middle of the night, you would always be able to see everything in your room and know where you were. Now that you are an adult, you don't need the night light anymore and assure them that they will know when that time is for them.

What you are doing is communicating to them that you heard their fear. In doing so, you validate their feelings and give them the hope that they too will grow out of it. The instructor stated if the adult is still afraid of the dark, tell your children that you still use a night light when you are sleeping because you like to see if you have to get up. She encouraged us not to accentuate the fact that you still have the fear itself, just that you are more comfortable sleeping with a night light on and that's okay to do.

The adult is effectively transforming the situation from feeding a fear to helping the child be part of finding a solution to the problem. I was learning that empowering children to problem-solve will eventually lead to less fear and help them gain confidence in feeling more control in the situation. This was all making sense to me. Good stuff I could use with my kids. Sometimes I could hardly wait to get home to start implementing what I was learning (and then I remembered the pie and coffee).

Did I mention that parenting was the most difficult job I had ever accomplished? Well, this is one of those examples. The above situation does not occur just once, never to happen again. I found myself out of bed several times, for all four children, with fears of the dark, storms or bad dreams. The alternative choice was to let all four children sleep with me and that was not a healthy or workable solution.

However, all that work produced a reward because what I was creating was worth the effort. By being patient and consistent, I was able to help my children gain confidence in being able to self-sooth. I was creating trust within my children in themselves and trust between each child and me.

This was the beginning of a lifelong trust.

This simple concept has been paramount in every relationship and friendship I have had. Even during a disagreement with my children, if I took the time to listen to what they said – and truly validated what they said – our resolution of the problem was so much easier to discuss because they felt heard. Naturally, it takes practice (and I'm still practicing). I utilize the same techniques during discussions at work or with a friend or spouse. If I feel validated, I at least feel heard and then I know I can continue discussing from that point on. If I repeat what the other person said to me, it doesn't mean I am agreeing with the views or the statement that person is making. So often this concept is misunderstood because we think if we repeat what someone else is saying, it means we are in agreement with that statement. That's not true. We're just repeating what we heard them say so we can validate their statement and try to understand their point of view.

With my children, it helped me to clarify that I may not agree but I wanted to repeat the statement to make sure I heard them correctly. Then it was my turn to speak my truth about what I needed in the situation. Asking my kids to repeat what they think I said, helped them to listen to my words. Then we began the process of negotiating and finding middle ground.

Guess what? It worked for me. And it worked for them too.

When I feel heard, I feel valued. I wanted my children to know they were heard and they were valued by me.

****

Building trust between parent and child begins early in childhood.

Chapter 9: We Teach Our Kids to Lie – What?

When a person is punished for their honesty,
they begin to learn to lie.   Shannon L. Alder

The parenting class continued to stretch my thinking. The instructor stated, "We teach our children to lie." Of course, I disagreed. I knew I didn't do that. It was just the opposite at our house, or so I thought.

The instructor told us that children want to please their parents. I knew this first hand. Children don't like it when their parents are upset with them. So far I was identifying with the instructor's message.

Therefore when parents ask, "Who broke the lamp?" none of the children want to say they did it. They know they'll be in trouble. So all of them say, "Not me; it wasn't me." Automatically, the children don't want their parents angry so they won't admit their mistake. Consequently, the lies begin.

Another light bulb moment for me.

The instructor explained that instead of asking the question which sets up the situation for our children to lie to us to stay out of trouble, we make an observation, a statement which tells the children we aren't going to be angry or upset with their answer.

That also meant as a parent, we had to decide if it was more important not to be angry over the broken lamp, in order to teach our children to tell the truth. The "Who broke the lamp?" question instead becomes, "I noticed the lamp is broken and I won't be angry if I can understand how it happened." If we continue to get angry over the broken lamps, etc., our children will continue to deny their involvement and the cycle continues.

I had already been asking questions like that of my children. After this particular class, I knew what the instructor had said applied to me – that common sense thing again.

At home when I saw spilled juice on the floor, instead of asking a question, I would state, "I see some juice has spilled on the floor."

Automatically, I heard four "wasn't me" responses. Naturally, they didn't want to be trouble.

"Oh, it must have been Kevin, my imaginary friend, because none of you said you did it."

The kids looked at each other like they knew I was crazy. I told them if none of them had spilled the juice then it must be someone else that lives in our home and that I would call him my imaginary friend, Kevin.

Then I would say, "If you see Kevin, tell him I am not upset he spilled his juice over here, but I would like him to wipe it up so it doesn't get tracked all over the floor because the juice is so sticky." And I let the rest go.

At first I think the kids were just glad they weren't in trouble and relieved I wasn't upset. That became the key to the solution.

I used the same tactic when I found something broken in the house. The kids gathered around and I would ask that if they saw Kevin upstairs to let him know I wasn't angry about the broken vase in the dining room but wanted Kevin to apologize for breaking it and then I would feel better.

Pretty soon one of the kids would come to me and say they had talked with Kevin upstairs. They would tell me that Kevin was very, very sorry about the broken vase, and he would never have pillow fights in the dining room again. Then I would hug him and tell him he must be very proud of himself for talking with Kevin and encouraging Kevin to tell the truth. We discussed that it takes a lot of courage to tell the truth if you think someone will be upset with you.

Then I would repeat the facts as I understood them. (Meanwhile, I was aware that other little ears were listening.)

"So Kevin and you were having a pillow fight and one of the pillows accidentally knocked over the vase." I kept stressing the part about how much courage it takes to tell the truth. It's difficult knowing you might disappoint someone or make someone angry if they know you broke something of theirs.

My goal was to teach them to tell the truth. I know I wouldn't have told the truth when I was their age if I knew I was going to be punished so I needed to give this a try.

It worked.

Reminding myself that, if the children told me the truth they would not be punished, became a constant phrase that was repeated again and again. When the kids came to me and told me they broke something (or Kevin did), I would remember to take a deep breath (several, actually) and hear what they were saying before I responded so I could respond in kindness. This took a great deal of practice and patience on my part… (a boatload in fact).

In my mind, I silently repeated, *Big picture… big picture…stay calm… what do I want them to learn from this? Let them speak their truth.*

I could tell their apology was sincere, and that they were admitting what they had done, so I knew we had both learned a valuable lesson. They could tell me the truth, and I learned I could hear them without overreacting and wanting to lecture them about what they had done, or worse yet, punish them.

Telling the truth is so courageous. I acknowledged how proud they must be of themselves for acting so bravely, which helped them to feel responsible for their behavior.

Big truth here for me: understanding that praising the child and acknowledging their actions are two different things. If I praise the child for doing something good or telling the truth, what I am actually doing is saying how happy my feelings are that the child behaved the way I wanted. I wasn't letting the child accept responsibility for their behavior.

If I acknowledge that I see how proud they must feel for telling the truth or ask how they feel about their behavior, the child is the one who identifies the feelings and claims ownership instead of trying to please the parent. Repeating over and over to myself, *acknowledge the child's actions and allow him/her to have ownership of the feelings of that behavior.* (If I could have, I would have taped those words to my tongue so those would be the first words out of my mouth.)

Practice, practice, practice. Another "P" word. Practice and Patience, both escaped me at times.

Starting this "Kevin thing" very early with my children definitely helped ease the tension when something was spilled or broken. It wasn't long before they were coming to me and telling me what "Kevin" did before I even had a chance to ask them or find out that something was broken or spilled.

They were learning at a very early age that telling the truth was very important, and that you feel good about yourself when you tell the truth.

What began as, "I just wanted to tell you that Kevin accidentally broke a plate today," quickly moved to, "I just wanted to tell you that I accidentally broke a plate today."

I continued to stress the importance of feeling good about themselves when they tell the truth and acknowledged their brave, courageous actions. I loved the fact that we had learned this behavior together.

Remember that saying, "Pick your battles?" I was relieved that I seemed to be yelling at the kids less... at least sometimes.

We used to laugh about Kevin's deeds all the time. Kevin "joined our family" when the children were very young – in elementary school. One day when the older kids were in middle school and high school, I came home from work and the kitchen was a mess (for the umpteenth time). The kids were watching a Cubs game on TV. I walked right past them to go upstairs and instructed them in an exasperated voice to clean up the kitchen while I changed my clothes so we could begin fixing dinner together.

Without missing a beat, Mike said in a "pretend" exasperated voice, "That Kevin! He made such a mess in the kitchen and then talked us into watching the Cubs game! He's always getting us into trouble."

We all burst out laughing. And by the time my clothes were changed, the kitchen was picked up and ready for the next round of food preparation.

I wish I could say I used this philosophy 100 percent of the time and that I never yelled or got upset. Both Kevin and I occasionally had trouble keeping our cool. However, this philosophy worked most of the time.

For the times I fell short, I was able to practice my apologies, which is something we also teach our children. How can we expect them to own their mistakes, when we do not accept responsibility for our own? When they receive an apology, it makes them feel important, valued, and that their feelings count. It shows them that we as parents have respect for them.

In my home, parenting was not going to be a one-way relationship. One-way relationships are power-based relationships where children feel their opinions are not important or valued. Teaching my kids the importance of the give and take in a relationship when they were young became even more valuable when they became teenagers.

As I was teaching my children to tell the truth, they were teaching me not to overreact to everyday situations.

Kids 1 – Mom 1

****

Learning to tell the truth in childhood becomes a lifelong habit.

Chapter 10: Just Trying to Survive

I've learned that you shouldn't go through life with a catcher's
mitt on both hands; you need to be able to throw something back.
Maya Angelou

One of the things that I did to survive when I was still married
and a stay-at-home mom was to have outside interests.
Volunteering in the emergency room of our local hospital became
a weekly night out for me. It was in the emergency room, seeing all
of the patients coming in for care, where my week would be put
into perspective. At home I felt like Mrs. Referee, settling tag team
fights. Now, I realized, their bickering was normal behavior and not
a big deal. Annoying, yes. Likely to change, no.

In the ER, I saw teenagers coming in by ambulance after a car
accident or elderly patients coming in to be x-rayed for broken
bones after a fall at a nursing home. Most came alone and most
were afraid. They all asked the same question, "What was going to
happen next?" The big unknown.

My job as a volunteer included many duties, but it was visiting
with patients or families while they were waiting that captured my
attention.

It was scary for patients to be waiting for treatment and
volunteers helped pass the time, letting them know they were not
alone. It meant talking with the teenagers until their parents arrived,
knowing I would want someone talking with my teenager if they
were ever in an accident. Not that I could change anything, but if
you have someone to share the pain and the fear with, sometimes
things are a little bit better. At times, just sitting quietly with them
until family members came was all that was needed.

I met some amazing people who taught me so much about life
and how I wanted to look and sound if it were me in that emergency
room waiting for test results or being admitted to the hospital. I

also knew that quietly visiting and listening to someone distracted their mind away from the pain and anxiety. They weren't carrying it alone.

I'll never forget one of the teenagers who had been brought in as the result of a car accident. He must have been 16 or 17 and was trying so hard not to cry or show any emotion. Asking if he was in pain, he replied, "I'm more worried about what my dad's going to say about the car – it's completely totaled."

I responded, "First, I bet he's going to be so glad to see you're alive, and then you can deal with the rest." I was right. That dad rushed to the bedside of his son to give him a huge hug.

I wish I could say every visit was that promising. Some ended differently. A few parents came but were annoyed and expressed those feelings to everyone. It taught me to change my words to the patient. Just asking if they would like some company while they were waiting seemed to fit better. I was no longer going to promise something that may not happen for them. Listening to whatever the teen wanted to talk about at the time was all I needed to do.

Most times, I just listened. My heart took notes for the days ahead with my own children.

It was staying with those teenagers and listening to them that helped me to know how teenagers think. When you come into someone's life in a crisis like the emergency room, you enter their lives at a very vulnerable time. They talked about what they were worried about, what annoyed them about school or their feelings about their families.

Sitting with parents in the waiting room, I listened to their fears of what might be wrong with their child and what the test results might show. Sometimes listening and validating their feelings were the only things I had to offer. And that was enough. It just felt like the right thing to do.

To become better equipped to deal with situations in the Emergency Room, I decided to take a Death and Dying class at our community college. Hoping it would help prepare me in case a patient in the ER passed away, I wanted to know how I could best help and what to say, if anything. Patients and families need someone to talk to during this traumatic time. The class taught me the best thing I can do is to listen. There isn't anything that I need to fix. I just needed to listen. And listen I did.

Unknown to me at the time, I was really taking a life-changing class that would be put into use immediately during my divorce and the years ahead. The professor stated that the number one cause of stress was death of a loved one. The number two cause was divorce. Our instructor quickly informed us that divorce ranked very close to the number one stressor, because there are always ongoing issues in divorce and some of those issues never get resolved. The stress can be a constant factor for years between the divorced couple. Stress can cause the body to become weaker and more susceptible to disease.

In class we learned that in death, we mourn the person who has passed. Usually within two or three years, we are able to begin to move forward, putting our loved one's memories into our hearts forever and carrying them with us throughout the rest of our lives.

We also learned when there are children involved in a divorce, your former spouse is always going to be involved in your life, because they are your children's other parent. Even if the other parent doesn't stay involved with the children, the kids struggle with abandonment issues. Either way, the stress of divorce will last much longer.

For me personally, I began thinking of the kids' ballgames, recitals, birthdays, graduations, weddings, etc. that both Jerry and I would be attending with our children. From what I had read, heard in classes, and learned from friends, there were war stories about divorces and what happens between the couple after they split up. The children get caught in the middle. Promising myself I would never put our children in the middle, there were still times I was tempted because of an issue between Jerry and me.

The vision of my children walking into a room where both Jerry and I are standing in opposite corners and the internal struggle for the children to decide which one of us to go to was enough for me to end putting the children in the middle. Keeping my word and respecting myself and honoring my children at all times became my goal. Whenever I felt like bad-mouthing Jerry or complaining about him in front of the kids, I would ask myself, *Is this fair to the children? How would I feel if I was the child in this divorce? Would I want to hear my mom complaining or bad-mouthing my dad or vice versa?*

Writing in my journal or talking with a good friend helped ease my stress and allowed me to keep my children from being caught in the middle.

This is one of the things that I am proud of...not bad-mouthing their father to my children and not putting them in the middle.

****

Volunteer work was a great release for me while going through my divorce. It took the focus from me and placed it on others. It expanded my mind and my heart. It connected me to the outside world in a giving way. I was expanding the role model I was presenting to my children and they benefitted by the volunteering as well.

Chapter 11: Whose Guidelines?

Who of us is mature enough for offspring before the offspring themselves arrive? The value of marriage is not that adults produce children but that children produce adults.
Peter DeVries

With my parenting classes over and the counseling sessions moving me to a place where I was feeling better about me, I decided it was time to put some guidelines down on paper to help me focus on what was important early in my divorce. The information I gathered about guidelines came from various sources, some from the parenting classes I took, some from the support groups I was involved in, some from my ongoing counseling discussions, and some from just trial and error. Finding what worked for our family of five was my goal. Common sense told me this was the right thing to do.

Guidelines helped my children settle into having two homes. Even if Jerry decided he didn't want to follow them, it was important to me that my children know these guidelines would always be enforced in my home. Guidelines helped me make my children feel safe. They were:

1. Don't badmouth the other parent. Ever! No name calling under any circumstances. Whenever I felt angry or frustrated, I confided in a good friend (or my counselor) who listened to my feelings. My children are half mom and half dad and if I criticized their dad in front of them, I would be condemning traits in my very own children. This could deeply hurt my kids and make them feel unloved. (This holds true for married families as well.)

2. Don't argue with your spouse in front of the kids. Our support group continually read the following messages each meeting: Be the adult and discuss differences away

from your children, even if you are the only adult who follows this guideline. Refuse to engage in arguments when your children are present. It takes two people to keep an argument alive; stop the conversation before it turns into an argument. Suggest meeting at a coffee house or restaurant so each of you can control your tone of voice more easily. Only discuss one topic at a time, resolve it and move to the next. Most times that worked.

3. Be honest – tell the children the divorce is not their fault. Tell them often. Everything I read confirmed that both parents should sit down with the children together and tell the kids at the same time that both parents are choosing to live in separate houses. I used age-appropriate books available for the children to read themselves and I read books to them about living in different houses. We read and re-read these books often as I needed the assurance that everything was going to be all right as much as they did.

4. Don't tell the details of why you are getting the divorce to the children. Together Jerry and I told the kids that we weren't able to live in the same house together because we couldn't agree on things and that when parents disagree about everything, it is best to live in separate houses. We then told our children the love for a child is a different feeling than the love of a spouse and that both of us would always continue to love our children and that the divorce was not their fault.

5. Children need the freedom to love both parents. I expressed to my children often that I wanted them to love both parents. To help my children understand this, I explained to the kids that their heart is like a puzzle and every person in their life has their own puzzle piece in their heart. No one will ever take the place of their mom or their

dad's puzzle pieces. They can always add puzzle pieces to their hearts when they meet new friends. That means their hearts are growing bigger, filled with more love each day. Tell them their dad's girlfriend or mom's boyfriend can be a new puzzle piece in their heart but no one will ever take the place of mom's puzzle piece or dad's puzzle piece. Giving my permission for them to love the other parent and the other parent's mate, gave them what they deserve because children want to love both parents.

6. Never use my children to pass messages (written or verbal), money or support checks to the other spouse. I will accept my responsibility as an adult and communicate with Jerry without using my children as a go-between. There is never a substitution for this rule.

7. Be respectful of time guidelines when picking up and dropping off our children with each other – give at least a half hour to an hour leeway time for traffic, etc. This allowed my kids the privilege of being happy to see their dad while saying goodbye to me. When the guidelines were stretched or broken, I would try to remember to make this less stressful for the children and act like the adult. I tried to discuss the guidelines alone with Jerry when the children weren't present and asked that he do the same. I didn't plan on meeting friends 15 minutes after the kids were picked up, so when Jerry was running late, I didn't have to become angry or frustrated in front of the kids (learned by example). This actually worked when I allowed the hour leeway time. If one parent is constantly checking their watch or anxiously waiting for the other parent to pick up the children because they have somewhere else to be, the children will receive the message that you are anxious to "get rid" of them. The kids and I usually did something fun together while waiting for their dad to pick up them up so the kids didn't feel anxious or worried. We played cards or

put puzzles together. I had to remember that I was the adult and accept that responsibility and model that behavior.

8. Have clothes, toys and games at both houses so the children feel each home is theirs. This was an important activity that I involved the children in so they would have a voice in dividing their toys, games and clothes for each home. Letting them make some of the decisions helped them feel ownership in their new home with belongings they selected. My two youngest children were still sleeping with a comfort blanket at night and did not have "the" blanket at their dad's house one weekend. That night my oldest daughter, Kelly, called from Jerry's home and said the younger kids were crying at bedtime because they wanted their blankets and asked me what she should do. Together we decided to give them soft towels for that particular night and when the two younger children arrived home the next day, we discussed a plan. Holding up their blankets, I asked if they would like me to cut them in half so they could have a blanket at each home. They both agreed and I let them help me cut the blankets and we sewed a hem down each cut edge. They happily took one of their new "blankees" to their new home with Dad. They helped find a solution for the problem.

9. Give my kids permission to have a good time at their dad's house. Kids worry about the other parent when they aren't with them and can feel guilty or responsible for the happiness of the other parent. If they're with dad, they miss mom and if mom cries when the children leave to go with dad, the children feel guilty. I had to be the adult and tell them that I wanted them to have a really good time with their dad and that I had a fun time planned too. This gave the kids the freedom to enjoy their visit with their dad and they didn't have to worry about what not to tell me when

they returned. At first I was jealous of all the things that the kids did with their dad and wished that I had the money to do the same things. Then I asked myself, *What do I really want the kids to experience when they were with their dad? Did I want them to be miserable, or angry because their dad was mean to them or sad because their dad never came to see them? Do I want them to hate their time with their dad?* No, I truly wanted the kids to have a good time with their dad (and they did). It was my job to embrace that good feeling for them and help promote the good times they would have together. I knew I would miss them but told them that we would both share our good times together when they returned. This helped them to trust that I'll be fine when they are at their dad's home. It also challenged me to create fun times when the kids were with me so that I felt I was having good times with them too. I didn't want to be known as Mrs. Drill Sergeant who made everyone clean their rooms and pick up their toys.

Here's an example: one night after dinner, I left the kitchen area but could still hear the children talking. What I heard was Kelly telling Mike not to tell me how great their weekend had been at their dad's home because she thought it would hurt my feelings. Fortunately, I was able to tell them I overheard their conversation and that I was happy to hear everything they did on the weekend. That allowed me to share my fun weekend with them as well. Wanting us to be able to share all of our experiences together helped us speak truthfully. Otherwise, the message to my children is that they have to hide part of their conversation and filter what they tell me so that my feelings don't get hurt. That means they are responsible for my feelings. I didn't want them to filter their experiences. Learning to be in charge of my own feelings helped me to be strong enough to hear all of their good times without feeling jealous. When I felt jealous (which I did), I learned to challenge myself to plan fun things that the kids and I could do together and that helped. It changed my focus from jealousy to something positive and fun. I thanked Kelly for thinking of my feelings and told her I hoped she felt good about herself for sharing her thoughts and thinking of others. I also expressed to all the children that I wanted them to talk about their weekends with their dad with me because that is their truth. They deserve to feel free to speak their truth.

10. Be consistent in the discipline in each of the homes. This is a really tough one. If that's not possible, here's what happened at our home. When one of the kids said, "but daddy lets me do that at his house," I found myself stating (over and over again) calmly but firmly: "I'm sorry that you have different rules at each of our homes but that is the way it has to be for each home. Your dad and I still love all of you children; however, we each have our own rules for our own homes. I know you will work hard to follow them." I used this opportunity to give them credit for having to learn the different rules at each home. I compared the different rules in each home to different rules in each classroom at school. Every teacher has his or her own rules to follow in their own classroom. Acknowledgement of my children's ability to learn new rules every year at school was discussed. This helped them feel needed in the support they gave to each relationship, their dad's and mine. The children needed to feel they were contributing to the new adjustments in making the whole family feel the situation was working. This made them feel included and helped affirm that they were still a valuable part of the family.

11. Ask the children if they would like to join a Kids' Support Group. I wanted to give my children an opportunity to meet other children who are experiencing some of the same feelings they were. This was an age appropriate

judgment on my part. I asked at the children's school if there was a kids' group who have divorced parents. (If not, ask the school social worker to start one so your children can be a part of it.) Take them to a group and let them have a couple of meetings to make up their mind. Maybe they will learn from others in the group or maybe they will teach others what they are learning and it will help them to know they are not alone. I shared with my kids that I had joined an adult support group and explained how it helped me. The bottom line was: many days I felt very alone and wondered if they did too. Talking about it together helped all of us.

12. Validate their feelings. All of us need to have our feelings validated. I knew if I didn't listen to my children's feelings, they would learn to bury their feelings or feel that they are not important enough to be heard. When they told me that they missed their daddy, I would repeat what they had said. "So you miss your daddy a lot, huh? What would make you feel better? Would you like to call him on the phone or draw him a picture?" That helped my children find what they needed to feel better. It was a way to help teach them to self-soothe. And when I validated their feelings, it told them that they had the right to feel the way they did and had a safe place to talk about it. Trying to help them to feel it was safe to tell me how they really felt, made me feel better. All of us deserve to feel safe and feel loved.

13. Wait a year before bringing someone new into my children's lives. We discussed this many times in our support group. The children and I were both still grieving and I knew all of us needed some time to heal and make some adjustments. Using that year to feel more comfortable in my new situation by having some counseling sessions, learning to love myself again and beginning an even stronger bond with my children helped

me feel more secure. When it did begin to feel right again, this meant dating other people when the children were at their dad's for the weekend. As time passed, on the weekends I had my children with me, I would meet my date away from home. Even though more than two years had passed, I knew this was still not the right time to bring someone new into their life. My inner voice would let me know.

14. Listen. And listen some more. The more I listened, the more I learned.

What started out as setting guidelines primarily for my children, ended up making me feel better about myself just by doing the right thing for both my children and me. Simply by writing down the guidelines, it made me focus on what environment I wanted to create in my home and writing them down seemed to engrave them in my memory. On the days that I was really struggling (and I had a lot of them), at the end of the day, I tried to remind myself of the positive things that worked that day and let the rest go.

The next day, I started over again.

****

As difficult as divorce is, we can best help our children by setting some ground rules for the adults to use during this time. Children feel safe when they know there are boundaries set in place. In the beginning, the parent has the power and gradually transfers some of that decision-making over to the child as they learn to get in touch with their feelings and begin to control their behavior. Guidelines and consistent discipline mean children learn that the parent cares enough to keep the child safe – and every child wants to feel loved and feel safe.

Chapter 12: Things I Wanted to Teach my Children (or so I thought)

Tell me and I forget, teach me and I may remember,
involve me and I learn.   Benjamin Franklin

Becoming a parent, and then a single parent, made me think about things I wanted to teach my children. However, they had a plan of their own. Picture me with my huge head, so big I can hardly carry it around, thinking I would be the one doing all the teaching and they would be following me around everywhere, hanging on my every word. Well, that never happened.

What kind of mom do I want to be?

I wanted to be the kind of mom who, years after the children left home, would find us all reminiscing about the fun times we had growing up.

My intention was to be remembered for doing the right thing and making a difference in their lives. Basically, I just didn't want to be known as Mean Joe Green or the Wicked Witch, even though, as a single parent, I quite often felt like a combination of both.

My kids taught me to stay connected to my sense of humor because we all made each other laugh and laughter made each day brighter. Years from now, in remembering the fun times when they grew up, they will know how to create that atmosphere when they have their own families.

I wanted my children to grow up laughing and teasing each other, using the kind of teasing where the person you are talking to feels good about what is being said to them and is laughing and smiling too.

The bad teasing is when someone is the butt of the joke and others are making fun of them. The receiver of this bad teasing doesn't feel good about himself and that kind of teasing is hurtful. We all know that's how bullying begins...in the home, and it's carried out at school in the hallways, on the playground and after school. The children who are bullied at home feel powerless. They become the bullies at school. It was my responsibility as a parent to stop the bullying in the home.

Every time my children were teasing each other in a mean way, I reminded them that no one deserves to hear cruel things said to them, and asked for the teasing to stop. They were typical children and had to be reminded many times. Using this opportunity, I discussed with them the effect of bullying and effective ways the children can help others who are bullied at school.

Explaining that bullies do not feel good about themselves and have to put others down in order to feel better, we discussed ways that they could help when they saw it happening in school. Saying, "That's enough" or "Leave him alone" or "Come on, let's go" or "Stop it" helps diffuse the situation.

The by-stander is the person who has the power to help redirect or deflect the bullying. Giving my children the tools to help alleviate the tension would help them to assist others when the bullying occurred. We did some role playing to help them practice speaking up for someone and what it might feel like to speak up.

Did I expect my children to reprimand the bully and address him directly? No, but I wanted to help them have words or actions that they could feel comfortable with to stand up for the person who was the target of the bully. I knew there were other children like mine, who felt this was wrong but didn't know what to do. My children now had more information concerning the issues. If one child can stand up and say, "Leave him alone," hopefully another friend can say, "Yeah, knock it off."

My children and I discussed what it would feel like to be the child that was bullied. We decided he would feel very alone if no one stood up for him. Standing up takes courage, but it's the right thing to do.

Role-playing and bullying discussions presented the perfect segue into discrimination conversations. We talked about diversity in simple terms. For me, this meant describing diversity as "differences in people," then we all listed the differences. We talked about all men and women being created to have equal rights, and in order to live by that statement it means our actions show other people what we believe. So if we are kind and caring to others and treat them all the same, we are showing that we believe we are all the same, regardless of our differences in race, religion, culture or sexual preferences. These conversations (when appropriate) continued at our dinners together and our bedtime talks.

It was important for me to have my children understand the importance of treating others with dignity and respect. They knew I had given them permission to not have to like everyone, but I expected them to treat everyone with respect. I was hoping my message would sink in and show in their actions, because it seemed on some days they couldn't even get along with each other. Other days, I felt like I was talking to the wall. But I just kept talking.

I knew I had to set daily goals for how I wanted to raise my children. Over the next several weeks, I created a list of the qualities I hoped my children would possess when they were adults and then created my goals from those qualities. It was my responsibility to develop the environment for that learning to take place. I wanted my children to grow up in a home with the following experiences:

- to be able to express their feelings
- to be heard
- to feel validated
- to have a voice in the solutions to problems
- to feel loved and valued
- to feel respected
- to laugh

Being the adult in this family circle (well, most of the time), my goal for the children was to respect my thoughts, ideas and suggestions, i.e. to do what they were told to do while still learning how to speak up for themselves without doing it rudely or in defiance. *Wow! Did I really think I could accomplish this?* The task at hand some days seemed overwhelming.

When I realized how valuable hearing their input was, I encouraged their participation. When I encouraged their participation, I learned the children were more engaged in accomplishing the task at hand because they felt important enough to be asked for their thoughts and ideas. As a single parent, when I found something that worked well for everyone, I continued to use it over and over.

Here are some of the things I learned along the way and wanted to pass on to my children:

1. Give time to yourself – always do something just for you each day. I learned (the hard way) that I could not give to anyone if I didn't have something within myself to give.

    For me, this meant little things like showering before any of the kids were up and having my coffee and reading the headlines of the newspaper. It sounds very basic but I learned to have the children join my day instead of me waking up to children needing help to get dressed for school, wanting breakfast, etc. and feeling like I was joining their day. Just by establishing this simple pattern, I felt more in control of my day.

    It meant planning something fun each day that I enjoyed as much as my children. I never felt I sacrificed because of the choices I allowed myself. It was this priority, to always take care of myself too, that I credit for getting me through the long, tough days. That and my positive attitude. It meant taking a vacation by myself for a few days when the children were with their father for the weekend. It meant packing up my favorite magazines, a good book, junk food and spending two days just being on my own schedule. It meant eating at a restaurant by myself. It was giving me permission to enjoy me. Short breaks from our routine worked for me.

It meant playing tennis once a week or enjoying card games with friends. Or joining a book club and actually trying to complete a sentence without being interrupted. Planning...it meant making fun things a priority for me. It was important that my children knew my time was scheduled with fun times too. I didn't want their role model to be a mom who just stays home and waits on everyone.

2. Speak up for yourself. This was a hard lesson for me. In counseling, I was learning the same thing. I wanted my children to know right away that you can speak up for yourself. No one can read your mind. Realizing that if I asked each one of the kids what they wanted, I could end up with four different answers. Preparing to negotiate a solution, I began asking the children what they wanted or needed and then had to be quiet and listen to their answers. Sometimes being quiet was hard for me because I wanted to give them a suggestion of what they might like because that would work best for all the rest of us (mainly me). I struggled in learning this. Visualizing keeping my mouth closed until they got their whole answer out, I wondered, *How could I do that?* The best thing I had around the house to fix things was duct tape. So I pictured myself with a roll of "imaginary duct tape" and each time I wanted to speak out when I should be listening, I would use a piece of my imaginary duct tape to cover my mouth. (I was thrilled that it was basic gray which blended nicely with every outfit I owned.) Thanks to my duct tape, I was able to take a deep breath and think about what to say before I charged into the conversation and found myself spouting off something that I would later regret.

The duct tape came to my rescue one night at dinner. My son, Mike, who was about age nine, was telling us about the great weekend the kids had spent with their dad and Jean, his new wife. Mike said Jean had served the best casserole

52

he had ever eaten and asked if I would call Jean and get the recipe. (Bring on the duct tape. And then breathe and breathe some more.) Thank heaven I had my mouth full of food and purposely spent a great deal of time chewing every morsel to a pulp, all the while trying to think of what my response could possibly be. I wanted to scream, *Are you frickin' kidding me? Call Jean for a recipe?* My sensor button kicked in, *Can't say that. Try again... He could be telling me that they eat junk food all the time or that Jean is a terrible cook but he wasn't saying any of those things. He was paying her a compliment.* Finally, I came up with, "Mike, if I called Jean for the recipe, you might get tired of having the casserole at both houses. Maybe you could tell Jean how much you love it and ask her to fix it a lot when you are at their home. Then you won't get tired of having it at both houses." Mike agreed that was a good plan. (*Whew! The pressure for getting the recipe was over.*)

I kept my imaginary duct tape handy during the entire time I was raising my children and continue to keep it nearby even today. At times, I have been known to remove it a little too quickly; however, overall I'm still glad to use it as a resource.

3. Apologize when there's been a disagreement with one of the kids or a friend so you can move ahead in the relationship. Explaining to the children that this doesn't necessarily mean I'm changing my mind and agreeing with them; it means I'm sorry we argued or disagreed about something. We may have to agree to disagree and resume our friendship. This acknowledges the disagreement so we can move on instead of ignoring it or pretending it never happened. No one has ever complained when someone apologized too soon – go ahead and be the first to say you're sorry. It feels good. We discussed this many times in our family of five.

4. Show people who you are everyday by being proud of your actions and taking responsibility for them. This is how I explained it to my children: Everyday people show us who they are by their words and their actions, and I have a choice how I respond to them. I've never been a person who believes in revenge, so if someone does something that hurts me or is insensitive, I automatically think "they are showing me who they are." The times that I get hooked into being upset by someone doing or saying something rude or insensitive is when I take the action or words personally. And during this divorce time-frame, I was definitely taking stuff personally. I had my work cut out for me. I worked at finding a way to set a boundary for myself so that I won't get caught up in it again. I learned their words and actions were about them, not about me. My focus became concentrated on doing what I had the power to change and moving past the things I cannot. I learned this from a wise counselor who helped me to focus on being true to myself and speaking from my heart. Sometimes I may be the only one who I feel knows the truth in that particular situation, and maybe that is all that is necessary at the time. If I know the truth for me and am proud of my actions, then I can be at peace with myself. This is something I practiced over and over and continue to work on every day.

5. We teach others how to treat us by our actions and by our words. My own childhood taught me that the way family members treat us affects us into our adult lives. As a people pleaser, I had enabled others to treat me that same way. My challenge was to break that pattern and change how my children treated each other so they would learn to be each other's friends. That became one of my goals: for them to be best friends. Some days, okay, most days, the goal was reduced to just being civil to each other! It was my job to figure out how we teach others to treat us every day as a family member.

This next story I am not proud of; however, it gave me the courage to choose another behavior, and everyone in our family benefited by the change. One night I was feeling particularly stressed, which I'm sure was related to the divorce, single parenting, new job or maybe a combination of all those things (ya think?). Anyway, I was yelling at the kids for leaving the kitchen in such a mess (surprise). I was going on and on telling them that I hated the mess (like they didn't already know that). This was not my normal behavior when I was still married so I think we were all shocked it was happening. On that particular day, I can remember using such a harsh tone of voice that when I looked at them, I saw fear in their eyes. What a horrible feeling: my own children being afraid of me. I had to leave the room. A deep sadness invaded my heart. Shame filled my soul. I was the same people pleaser who rarely raised her voice, and now I had crossed a line.

When I returned, I apologized to them for yelling so loudly that they were afraid. I asked for their help; I told them we were a team and we had to work together. I asked if they could remind me to talk to them in a "nicer voice" when they heard me yelling. (Somehow I knew the yelling would happen again.) They still stood frozen, afraid to speak. I pleaded with them by adding, "I need your help. Please help me do this." Still silence. Finally my oldest daughter, Kelly, quietly confessed she didn't think any of them would be able to talk when I was yelling that loud. She said the only place I should yell that loud would be in the desert where no one could hear me. A wave of nausea spread over my body. My children were so frightened that they were afraid to speak while I was yelling. Her words confirmed my feeling that no one deserved to be yelled at as I had just yelled at my very own children, the people I loved the most in the whole world.

It was then we invented our code word, "desert," to be used if I was yelling. I asked them to find the courage to say that one word, "desert," and I would automatically know that I was yelling too loud. They hesitantly agreed to try.

It was only a few days later that I had slipped into another yelling episode and just as I was beginning to fire off another sentence, I heard this quiet, tiny voice behind me say, "desert." I quickly spun around to see who had spoken, and all eyes were on me... eyes filled with fear that now someone would really be in trouble. My heart ached. Once again I saw the fear in each of their eyes. *How could I have created this in my own children?* I felt ashamed of my behavior. I immediately slapped my imaginary duct tape over my mouth and began to breathe, long deep breaths. Slowly peeling off the duct tape, I thanked them for having the courage to use the code word as the reminder that I was yelling. Then I told them I needed a little time to calm down and left the room. Tears spilled down my cheeks. *How could I treat my children so horribly?* Shame reared its ugly head again.

What do I want my children to learn from this? How can I help them trust me? How do I quit yelling? Returning shortly and much more relaxed after visualizing what I needed to do, I apologized again for my yelling. Then I thanked them for helping me. If they had not helped me by having the courage to say the word "desert," I would have taught them to be afraid of me. They would have never trusted that they would be safe with me.

Today, it is even difficult for me to admit that I yelled like that and I'm certainly not proud of my behavior. The gift of the story is that I did see what was happening and made the choice to find a way to change my behavior. In the process, the children discovered I needed their help and their support in learning a new behavior, and we felt a stronger bond as a family.

Out of my weakness came a huge family strength. We were a team.

Fast forward several months (and embarrassingly enough, many "desert" reminders later). Walking through the family room, I mentioned to the children that a friend was stopping by later and asked them to please pick up their things. Mind you, I had used my nice voice. As I turned and started up the stairs, I heard the word "desert." My head spun around because, in my opinion, my voice was in no way the harsh yelling tone that I was known for in the past. What I saw was a little grin on Mike's face. I was so shocked that he was teasing me about something that had been so hurtful to all of us, and then instantly, we all burst into laughter. As we laughed, I knew the healing had begun for all of us.

6. At the end of the day, telling each child one thing they did or said that I was grateful for that day made each child feel special. The deed was specific and each day was something different. Some days, it seemed like a stretch to try to find something nice because I was only recalling their fights with each other. (I wanted to say, "Thank you, kids, for stopping the fights right before I had to call the police".) Focusing on their positive behavior helped me remember something good. I was trying to let them know that each day they were valued. I loved tucking them into bed every night. Bedtime was a wonderful time to let them continue telling me what was on their mind. Giving a five or ten minute backrub was a great way to establish a connection with each of my children and touching was beneficial to both of us. This was pillow talk between mom and child. They each loved the alone time and each one felt special. So did I.

7. Every day my children received hugs from me. Hugging was
    not a part of my childhood and I wanted to change this for
    my children. All of us need to be hugged and when we learn
    how comforting hugging can be at an early age, we learn to
    trust and know that it feels good, and can accept hugging
    from others when we are older. When my two boys reached
    middle school age, they naturally became more
    independent. If I would ask them if they needed a hug, they
    would respond by saying, "Are you kidding? No, I don't
    need a hug." Then I would say, "You may not need it, but
    I do; so do your mom a favor and give me a hug." They
    would go through the motion but the hug would be limp
    and weak. Then I would imitate them, "This is what your
    hug feels like" and show them the weakest movement I
    could, barely touching them. They would laugh and take it
    as a challenge. "Oh, so you want a bigger hug," they teased.
    They responded by squeezing me so tightly that I thought I
    would stop breathing. This became one of the family jokes.
    They would give such strong hugs after that, it would
    almost make me choke. When I protested or gasped for air,
    they would say, "Oh, we thought you were choking and
    needed the Heimlich maneuver." They would both practice
    the Heimlich maneuver on me and all three of us would be
    laughing (while I'm gasping for breath). But I did get my
    hugs in one form or another.

8. It was important to make sure my children always knew I
    was happy to see them. They knew by the look in my eyes
    how welcome they were in my presence. We learned to play
    together even if it was a short time during the day, and by
    giving them my undivided attention it made them feel
    important. This early playing together helped set the tone
    for the difficult, crazy teenage years.

9. Giving to others was an example I tried to live by and wanted to pass on to my children. Several times throughout the year, we donated food to our local food pantry. Letting them pick out some of the favorite foods and talking about giving it to others was a good way for them to understand how the food pantry helped our community. We delivered Meals on Wheels and helped deliver baskets of food and presents for Christmas Clearing House. The kids would help me make soup and deliver it to someone who was recovering from a recent hospital visit. We made cookies together and delivered them to elderly neighbors. They enjoyed it as much as I did.

10. Most importantly: I tried to listen, listen, listen to my children at every age. Sometimes all a child needs is a good listening to.

****

Identify the characteristics that you want your children to have as adults. Then model those qualities in your own home. Children learn what they live.

Chapter 13: Whining, Begging and Other Super Annoying Childhood Behaviors

What you permit, you promote!
Arlene Pollock LaQuey

Did I mention that raising children can be exhausting? In order to feel some control over the situation, I learned to solve problems by starting with the ones that irritated me the most. There were three behaviors that I had a difficult time tolerating during the early years when the children were growing up. They were:

1. whining
2. yelling "me first" when it was time to do something
3. begging, i.e., asking me for something and immediately begging for an answer: "Can I, Mom, huh? Can I? Huh, Mom, can I? Please, let me go, can I?"

All of these situations drove me craaaaazzy. I knew I had a challenge on my hands because every child exhibits those three behaviors.

Tackling the "me first" by making the rule that whoever yelled "me first," would always go last, resolved that issue. It was explained that it was never used as a punishment to go last, but instead as a reminder that it is selfish behavior to always want to be first. That eliminated the "me first" immediately. The child who yelled "me first" was asked to help think of different techniques for who could go first. In trying to make it fun we came up with different suggestions, such as whose birthday was coming up next or who could guess what I was describing in the room. By the time I started passing out the snack, they were more involved in the conversation and didn't care who was first. It didn't take them long to start making up stuff on their own, such as "whoever is wearing something red can go first" or "whoever can spell Mississippi." As they were all giggling over the "i-s-s-i-p-p's" and getting each other mixed up, they forgot about being first. This method used fairness and encouraged creativity and sibling bonding. It became a game to see who could come up with a clever answer. Guess what? That was fun for me too.

The whining took me a while to work through because they all did it and it's a tough habit to break... four times. What worked best for me when they began whining, was to kneel so I could look directly into their eyes and say, "I'm sorry that I can't understand you when you're whining, but if you would like to ask me in another voice, I know I can help you." If they continued to whine, I would again say, "I'm sorry. I can't hear you in that voice."

With four children, I must have repeated that 50 billion times, but eventually they stopped whining and would make their request in their regular voice. It was interesting because over time, just as I knelt down and began saying, "I'm sorry that..." they immediately interrupted me with their same request in their regular voice.

Without even knowing it, they taught me to slow down, stay in the moment and continue to focus on listening to what was important at the time. Once again, we learned as a team.

Repeatedly asking for the same thing, the "Can I go, Mom? Huh, can I? Can I go, please, Mom, can I, can I?" behavior was also a challenge (which really means, it drove me absolutely nuts). It forced me to come up with a new strategy. When one of the kids asked for something that needed some thought, the rule became that once they asked me, I would set the stove timer for 15 minutes and if they asked me again before the stove buzzer went off, then the answer was always going to be "no." I explained I needed time to think about how it would involve the whole family, if we were going somewhere, previous plans, etc. I also explained that they could look at the stove timer and always know how long they had until they could ask again.

This taught the children some self-control.

I learned to focus on getting an answer for them (within that 15-minute time period) so they would not keep begging for an answer. This helped me to be a little more organized. This I learned through trial and error because at the beginning (before using the stove timer), the first child that asked me if they could have a friend over would automatically get a yes and then two seconds later, another child would come in and ask to have a friend over, and pretty soon I had eight kids at my house. Crazy settled in.

This solution of setting the stove timer for 15 minutes worked for us. Not only did the children feel heard as their question was being considered, I was given time to reflect on our day's schedule before committing to anything.

This simple technique also helped the kids to learn patience and self-control. When they would come running into the kitchen to ask the same thing they had just asked me, all I had to do was point at the stove before they could utter a word. They would know immediately how long they had to wait. Ultimately, this cut down on them begging me for something. Whew!

****

Setting specific behavior boundaries were ways for my children to receive guidance without feeling nagged. They understood what was expected of them. Consistency worked for both of us. They learned self-control while I was feeling more organized in the day's activities. More teamwork in action.

Chapter 14: What Part of 'No' Don't You Understand?

One of the biggest challenges was the children's overall behavior when we were going somewhere. I definitely wanted it to be fun for me and of course for them. This premise led me to set a boundary early on that I reinforced several times right at the beginning, and they quickly learned I meant business. If we had been invited over to a friend's home with other moms and children for the morning, I explained to them that they would get to play with their friends, and I would get to play with my friends. However, if they were fighting with their friends while we were visiting, then we would come home early.

Naturally, they pushed the limits on that one several times because kids fight. The first time one of the children began fighting with another friend, was a warning, then I listened to their ideas on how to share the toy, etc. or how each of them thought it could be resolved fairly. They always had a solution (they were used to doing this with their brothers and sisters).

Sometimes I would stay with the children awhile to observe the play and would talk with any of the children, my friends' children included, who were not playing fair. Then I'd say to all the children playing together they would have another opportunity to share this toy and play together and have fun or we will have to go home early. The minute the fighting broke out again, the children and I would go home.

It only took two or three times of leaving early, before they all learned I wouldn't compromise this rule. Not only did my children learn about boundaries, their friends and each one of my kids learned to share toys with fair guidelines (most days).

This guideline was for children three years of age or older. Children younger than three have a very difficult time sharing and interacting with others. When my kids were younger than three, I kept the group to one or two other children, and the other mom and I would sit on the floor and talk so the children would interact some and play on their own some. The children had easy access to both moms and could snuggle for a while and then get back to playing.

Setting the stove buzzer at friends' homes if their children were not sharing helped make it fair for everyone. The timer was a good way to make sure everyone had a turn with the favorite toy. Children understand fairness. Employing simple ways to create fairness, like a timer, meant I didn't always have to be the bad guy. This was a solution the children could easily follow or suggest themselves and helped make them feel in control.

Trading babysitting mornings with moms whose parenting styles were similar to mine worked for both the kids and me. When our children played together, they learned to play fairly and have a good time together while I was out enjoying my morning alone. With similar parenting styles, it also meant I had a good time when it was my turn to have all the children at my home while my friend had time to herself. This meant planning activities the children and I would do together. It was a great way to make sure everyone had fun and then I had some alone time when the children had an afternoon rest time.

It was so important for me to play with my children, not just send them off to play by themselves. The first 12 years I was home, I spent time every day playing games, cards, jacks, hop scotch, checkers, reading books and going for long walks with the kids. When I was interacting with my children, I was listening to what they were saying. They felt important and included in my life. We read books every day, went to the library and put puzzles together.

Over the years, I probably played with more than a truckload of play dough (I may still have some under my fingernails if I look closely). While playing together with my children, they learned about values, taking turns and developing their communication skills. What I learned was to have fun and stay connected to my inner child.

It was the same rule for going shopping. The explanation was given that we wouldn't buy candy, gum or toys every time we went to the store. That was the guideline. For me, it was much more about my children learning self-discipline than it was about eating a candy bar in the checkout line. Heck, I would've liked to eat a candy bar every trip to the store – bring on the Snickers and Heath bars.

At times, it seemed like it would have been so much easier to give in to the whining, cajoling and begging. However, that would have rewarded the children's behavior and reinforced the concept that they should whine and beg whenever they want something. My job was to change the subject and redirect their behavior away from the candy, gum, the "I-want-it-and-I-want-it-now" item. That meant asking for their help in unloading the cart unto the checkout counter, asking about what their favorite food was in the cart or playing rhyming word games with each item they pulled out of the cart. Anything that kept them entertained worked.

I learned from the parenting books and classes that children need guidelines, as they feel safe and secure when they know the boundaries. Children need parents who are loving and can hold firm when the boundaries are challenged. My children learned to respect me as a parent when I said no and meant no. They were also learning self-control.

When my children were young, there were as few rules as possible and the negotiating began when the child was age appropriate. In the beginning, the guidelines were:

- Treat others like you would like to be treated.
- No name-calling.
- No swear words and no potty humor.
- Only one half hour of TV per day per child. (There were no TVs in their bedrooms.) The rest of the time they played games with each other or neighbors, read books, played dress-up, anything but TV. There were definitely fun exceptions, like when the whole family watched a movie or the Cubs or Bears game – and watching for a

longer period of time was a treat and a privilege, not an everyday routine. This rule lasted until about middle school age and then the negotiations began for longer TV viewing. The children earned more TV privileges by accepting more responsibility in doing the chores around the house.

Responsibility was the key for guiding my children to success. In our home, privileges were earned. The more responsibilities my children chose to accept as their role of a team member, the more privileges they acquired. Their behavior guided their success or failure. And over time, they learned to own the feelings that came with each decision.

When the children were elementary age, the expectations were:
- Each child was responsible for cleaning their own room.
- Each child was responsible for picking up the toys in the family room area.
- Each child was assigned one week of clearing the table after meals and loading the dishwasher.
- Each child was assigned one week of helping prepare meals, setting the table, cutting up vegetables, etc. This became a wonderful conversation time between the two of us.

When the children were middle school age, added expectations were:
- Each child packed their own school lunch.
- Each child was responsible for cleaning the bathroom after showers, baths, etc.

When the children were teenagers in high school, the expectations added were:
- Each child added cleaning two more rooms in our home in addition to their own room.

- Each child did their own laundry. When Mike was a freshman in high school, he was used to his older sister, Kelly, doing her own laundry and when I told him that he had earned the privilege of doing his own laundry, he stared at me and said, "Laundry is for girls to do, not boys." He was serious. The kids were all in the room and everyone waited to hear how this challenge would go over. I smiled and said, "Laundry isn't just for girls. If I keep doing your laundry, then I'm going to have to go to college with you and share a room. We'll all have to order pizza together with your college friends because I'll be there to do your laundry and...". Mike started smiling and interrupted me saying, "I get it. Show me where the stuff is." I never washed a high school sports uniform, which took me out of the bad guy slot when the uniform was still in the gym bag from the day before. Not to mention, I secretly loved hearing the other mothers complain about the constant washing of uniforms and trying to get the stains out, knowing I didn't have to deal with that issue.
- No drinking alcohol.
- No drinking alcohol and driving.
- No driving out of town when the roads are icy.
- Call home if you will be late for curfew – this is the rule that was negotiated the most and depended on the circumstances, the child's age and how responsible they were at that time.

My oldest daughter, Kelly had the worst of the curfew situation, as I did not negotiate very much when she was in high school. She taught me a valuable lesson by her persistent determination that she deserved for me to listen to her requests. Her behavior proved over and over that she was responsible. She taught me that being flexible with curfew could be a reward for her responsible behavior. I just had the rigid rule mindset going at that time and was extremely difficult to persuade. (The word "stubborn" somehow comes to mind.) The other three children benefited from all of her negotiations.

I was still learning.

****

Children who have chores around the home learn responsibility and feel included as part of a family team. Being acknowledged for a job well done leads to a feeling of self-accomplishment and promotes self-esteem.

Chapter 15: The "F" Word

Some of the guidelines I enforced right from the beginning when the children were young had to do with language and things I learned from my childhood. The children weren't allowed to call each other "stupid" or "ugly" or anything degrading. (Those little darlings...would they ever think of such a thing? Pfffff.. sometimes before I was even out of earshot.)

Whatever our personal image of ourself is, that's how we feel others see us as well. If we allow others to call us names, such as stupid, dummy, idiot, etc., then pretty soon we make the connection in our head that the only people who do stupid acts are stupid people. If we are called "stupid" often enough, we begin to believe that maybe we are stupid.

If we don't have a good self image, when someone gives us a compliment, we are unable to hear it or accept it because our inner voice tells us that the people who really know us, day in and day out, say we are stupid. Then we say to ourselves, "Maybe the individual who just gave me a compliment doesn't really know me that well at all." The person retreats inwardly because he or she doesn't want others to see that stupid side, the one that our family must see because they call us stupid all the time.

Another one of the guidelines was not allowing any of us to use the words "shut up." Did they use it on each other when I wasn't around? Of course, but it was my job to plant the seed again and again that "shut up" wasn't allowed, labeling it as rude behavior.

Kids are kids. They all call each other names. So when my children called each other names, and if it was in my presence, I would remind them their brother or sister did not deserve name-calling. Because I was home with my children for the first 12 years, this became a constant reminder, and I was very tuned in to what they were saying to each other.

If you set the intention early enough, it becomes a habit, and they begin correcting themselves. For instance, if one of the kids said to another, "That was a stupid thing to do," I would say, "and you probably meant to say it was a mistake because we all make mistakes."

And after I left the room, I'm sure one of the kids mouthed "stupid" to the other one and not to be outdone, the other one mouthed back "shut up." They were, after all, kids.

When the children went to school and started with the potty humor, I explained we would not be using those words because they weren't polite. In using our good manners, we didn't want that word to be part of our vocabulary, or we would get into a habit of using it and say it all the time. Having good language skills was important so we would feel comfortable when we spoke. That's how we respect ourselves and respect others. I'm sure they used all of the swear words when I wasn't around. At least I think they were normal.

Friendly reminders worked much better than harsh punishment because it prevented the swearing from becoming a big taboo and even more tempting. Because I remained calm and firm, the kids took me seriously.

One evening when Kathy, age five, and Nick, age seven, were brushing their teeth while getting ready for bed, I heard this blood-curdling scream. Flying up the stairs, I couldn't imagine what had happened.

Kathy was crying so hard she could hardly catch her breath and Nick was calmly brushing his teeth beside her. Quickly assessing the area for blood, injuries, etc., I asked him what happened and he said, "Kathy said the 'F' word."

Then she screamed even louder. As I was trying to calm her down, I was instantly angry, thinking, *I'll bet she learned the "F" word from her brothers and she was probably teaching her kindergarten friends the "F" word at school. Great! Now I'm going to be receiving a call from the kindergarten teacher.*

Deep breath. Asking Nick what they were talking about, I tried to make sense of this scene. *What would make her say the "F" word?* I couldn't imagine.

Nick matter-of-factly stated that they were brushing their teeth and he burped, and then Kathy said, "That sounds like a fart." It was then Nick told her that he was going to tell Mom that she said the "F" word. That's when she started screaming.

Inside I wanted to burst out laughing. I could tell that Nick was pretty pleased with himself that he was going to be reporting her to the authorities for her audacious behavior.

Inside my head, I was doing cartwheels. This was the "F" word they were talking about.

Trying not to laugh, I calmly said, "Well, we all make mistakes," acting like it was no big deal. I could barely keep a straight face.

Just by using a calm voice, Kathy had already stopped crying. She could tell everything was going to be all right by the look in my eyes and the sound of my voice. Once she heard my voice was not an angry one, she finished brushing her teeth. We talked about how sometimes we say things by accident or as a mistake and we don't say those words all the time.

I assured her I knew she wouldn't say the "fart" word on purpose or to be rude. I told her that sometimes I think burps do sound like farts. We giggled with each other. Just saying the word "fart" made us laugh. Love that potty humor. I told her we could help remind each other when we forget and use a swear word. That's why we are family, to help each other.

Being a team that helps each other even when we make mistakes was the most important feeling I wanted to get across to her. She was more than happy to know I wasn't angry, and I could tell by her reaction she was sincere in her words of apology for using the "F" word.

Of course, in my mind, I'm smiling as I knew in the years ahead, the word fart would become one of the many words to use behind my back when they were with friends or their siblings. I would be referred to as "old fart face," along with a host of many others. But for now, at the young age they were, this was the appropriate message for the day. And of course, I couldn't wait to share the story with my friends over coffee.

Even in high school, the kids were respectful with their language and their use of swear words around adults. I know with their friends, it was a different story, but the important message we learned was when to use the swear words and when they were appropriate.

****

As the parent, we role-model for our children. Training children to use respectful language teaches them to respect themselves and others. Name-calling is a cruel and abusive behavior and needs to be addressed by the parent. Anything we do 21 days in a row becomes our habit.

Chapter 16: Everything I Always Wanted to Know, I Learned Around the Dinner Table...

Imagine working all day in a school with more than 650 children ages six through 12 and coming home to homework, practice schedules, friends and four children vying for my attention. On top of that, there was always another dinner to prepare...

So what do you fix when your brain is already scrambled? I learned early on that what we ate for dinner was not as important as what conversation occurred at the dinner table. In the beginning, when it was just the children and me for dinner, the two older children took over the dinner conversation and chatted about what had happened at school that day, etc. Soon I noticed that the two younger children, Kathy and Nick, ages four and six, were not talking that much. I began to wonder if they always felt like they had to fight for the few sentences they could eek out before being cut off by the constant conversation of Mike and Kelly.

That led me to begin our dinner table topics. Every night we ate dinner together at the table, never in front of the television. Each night at dinner, we would go around the table and say one good thing and one bad thing that happened to us that day. It was a great way for me to introduce good manners, which became habit forming. For a while, brief reminders were given about the rules at the beginning of each dinner so we all knew what to expect. As time went on, the rules became habits and didn't even need to be mentioned. We quickly slipped into the fun conversation. The rules were:

1. Whoever was speaking had the floor and there would be no interruptions.
2. No one could talk with food in their mouth.
3. We all had to chew our food with our mouth closed.

4. Everyone stayed at the table until all of us had a chance to tell our one good thing and one bad thing that had happened to us that day.
5. No phone calls during dinner.

I talked with Kelly and Mike separately before we began this "good thing, bad thing" conversation at the dinner table. My reasons were this: I explained to the older two that Kathy and Nick were not ever getting a chance to talk at the table and I wanted them to be outspoken like their big sister and brother and to speak out in class. If Nick and Kathy weren't comfortable doing it at home, they certainly weren't going to be comfortable once they were in school. I told them I needed their help.

Kelly and Mike understood immediately – I was praising them for being leaders in their classrooms and they liked the feeling. They felt important and were excited to be included as part of the development of conversation for their younger two siblings. They liked feeling needed in the family.

I also explained that if Kathy and Nick are laughed at and made fun of for the things they share at the table by Kelly and Mike, then the younger two will learn that home is not a safe place to share your feelings. I continued to tell each of the older children I needed their help in guiding the two younger children so they would feel safe and heard, too. Both were important. Explaining to them that Kathy and Nick looked up to Kelly and Mike and that they would become even more important role models as time went on held their attention. Both of the older children accepted the role and wore it very well... to the point of competing over the attention of the younger two. (Like I needed another problem, right?.) However, this was a good thing – most of the time.

Our dinner conversations were wonderful. We continued this practice for years until high school sports schedules and games changed our mealtimes. It was an easy way to catch up on what happened with everyone that day and we all looked forward to our dinners together. Anything repeated 21 times in a row, becomes a habit, and for us, our dinner table conversation was a great habit.

(While doing research, I discovered information from the National Center on Addiction and Substance Abuse at Columbia University that shows teenagers who reported eating two or fewer dinners a week with family members were more than one and a half times as likely to smoke, drink or use illegal substances than were teenagers who had five to seven family dinners.) Yeah for family dinners!

It was also a very effective way to work on teaching manners in a group so that we were all learning them together and someone wasn't constantly feeling like they were being picked on or yelled at for something.

Using a fork as a pretend microphone, or using an accent, I would quickly review the dinner table rules. Adding, thank you for listening and our first speaker this evening will be … drum-roll please, Miss Kathy, please tell us about your day…"

We had fun experiments when we would spend one minute where all of us would talk with food in our mouths all at the same time. It was pretty gross but it was also funny, and fun to just be silly together…either that or just completely nuts (probably a little of both). It helped to make this enjoyable for me, as teaching good manners didn't have to be a chore. I laughed just as much as the kids.

Sometimes they would ask if we could all talk at the same time when one of their friends was over for dinner. Their friends were shocked at first because it does get a little crazy. Their friends kept looking at me thinking I was going to get angry because the kids were all yelling and out of control and when I was doing it too, they started laughing with the rest of us. At times I wondered if their friends went home and told their parents that we all talk at the same time and with food in our mouth at dinner. Those Kaminski kids – doesn't their mother teach them good manners?

Another topic we added to the dinner table conversation was taking turns telling something new we learned that day. It was gratifying to see how excited the children were to share something new they had learned. They were the perfect example that learning can be fun. The kids were so caught up in listening and sharing their information with each other that they forgot they were learning social skills and the mastery of good communication at the same time.

The "something new I learned" conversation or the "good thing, bad thing" was a great tool for me to bring up with each child at bedtime and reinforced to each one of them that they had been heard and were an important contributor to our family.

****

The goal to have enjoyable dinner conversations and learn both good manners and social skills at the same time worked for all of us. It was safe and it was fun. Children learn more quickly when the learning is fun.

Chapter 17: Kathy Loves Two Moms

One night while tucking my six-year-old daughter, Kathy, into bed and giving her a hug, she said, "I'm so lucky because I have the best two moms in the whole wide world."

Fortunately my face was close to her pillow, because I felt like a knife went into my heart. I just kept thinking, *Keep your mouth closed; just say goodnight and get out of there.* I did just that.

Heading straight for my bathroom, I sobbed into a towel so no one would hear me. Two moms?

My mind raced with memories. Thinking about all the times the kids have been sick, and how I stayed up most of the night with them, comforting them and being exhausted the next day, knowing that one of the other kids would come down with the flu the next night, I wept until there wasn't a tear left to fall.

I thought about all the times the kids' fighting would get on my nerves and how I used every ounce of patience I had to help them mediate the issue. I tried to make sure there was time for each one of them because I wanted them to be heard and feel important and validated.

I wondered how someone could come into their lives, and in such a short amount of time, be considered my equal.

The long and short of it was: I was jealous. How could someone come into their lives and automatically be placed in the same category that I had spent the past 13 years trying to achieve? I felt angry, hurt and devastated.

Eventually, when I calmed down, I began to look at the other side of the coin. *What would I have wanted Kathy to say instead? That she was afraid to go to her dad's house because his wife, Jean, was mean to her or hit her or yelled at her? Would I have wanted Kathy to say she was afraid to go because her dad and Jean left them alone all the time? Or came home drunk or worse?* Having this conversation with myself, I knew why Kathy felt the way she did.

She felt totally loved by Jean, her new step-mom.

I knew I had a choice. I could continue nursing the jealousy that I felt and try to convince Kathy that I was her real mom and compete with Jean for Kathy's love, or I could look at my daughter's face and see her smile and hear her voice when she talked about being loved by her two best moms.

I knew what I needed to do.

Strange as it sounds, it actually felt good to know that my children were loved by their new mom, Jean – in such a short time – and that Jean had done everything she possibly could to make the children feel loved and welcomed. When you love your children, the only people you want around them are other people who are going to love them and treat them with kindness. That's what Kathy was trying to tell me. That when she went to her dad's home, she was surrounded by two people who loved her as I did.

Slowly, feeling relieved and embracing the thought that she is loved in both homes, I began to feel happy for the children. And wasn't that my original message to my children when they went to their dad's home… to add Jean as a puzzle piece to their hearts?

Not only had Kathy already done that, now she was teaching me to add Jean as a puzzle piece to my heart.

I went back into my daughter's bedroom just to give her another hug and kiss goodnight, and she was still awake. "I just came back to give you a big hug because you are so loved by both of your moms."

Kathy said, "Well, it's really my mom and my step-mom."

That was when I assured her that she was right the first time. She is loved by both her moms, and that she did have the best two moms in the whole wide world.

Earlier, I had heard the older kids talking about how cool their step-mom was. They said she dressed in cool boots and jeans and had a totally "in" hairstyle. I automatically assumed she had tons of time to spend primping and shopping for the latest fashions. I was already a little jealous that she had more free time than I did. I had just enough time and energy to look "sane," let alone "cool." Somehow, I couldn't imagine the kids at their dad's house talking about how cool I looked in my hot pink sweat suit.

My six-year-old daughter taught me and showed me that night what love actually felt like. Not the jealous version I was feeling as she was talking about her step-mom as her mom, but the real love that is felt between people who really care about each other.

By allowing me to witness her truth, my daughter had just taken me to a new depth of love I had not experienced before. I liked the way it felt. I liked the way it made me think in a whole new light. I liked the way it made me feel about my divorce and Jerry's new wife and my children's new other mom.

And I liked the way it made me feel about me – and that was "cool" too.

****

Because our children love unconditionally from the very beginning, they teach us invaluable lessons along the way. Our job is to be open to learning and growing, and to be able to step outside of ourselves to look at the big picture and what is best for everyone. Knowledge is power.

Chapter 18: Tired of Being the Bad Guy

One Sunday afternoon, I threw up my hands and said, "I can't do this anymore."

The kids just stood around looking at me, not quite knowing what to do. I had made plans for all of us to do something really fun (or what I thought would be really fun), and that was to go roller-skating on a Sunday afternoon.

Just before we were ready to go, one of the kids said, "I don't really feel like going roller-skating. I'd rather stay home and play here." I just wanted to pull my hair out because this situation happened a lot. Not being able to leave the child home alone, I would end up forcing the child to go somewhere he/she didn't want to go and that didn't feel right either.

This situation occurred over and over. These events were planned with the intention of having fun. Something was desperately wrong with this picture.

My tears flowed freely. Trying to stop them didn't work as they seemed to be connected to a faucet with no shut-off valve. Remembering that the children eagerly went along and participated whenever their dad took them for the weekend of fun activities, I couldn't figure out if they just didn't want to go with me or was it just this particular activity or what?

Whatever the problem was, this scene became the day the floodgates opened. The kids were staring at me, wondering what they should do.

Slowly, pulling myself together, I said, "We are all a family and when we go somewhere, it is important to me that all of us want to go together as a family and have fun with each other. I need your input and ideas. I need your help as family members because I can't do this alone. It's not working."

I knew it was true and I wanted them to feel a part of the commitment of belonging to this family. I had their attention (they were probably afraid if they didn't listen, I'd still be crying). Explaining that everyone's ideas are important and valued, we began to decide as a family what we would do the following week and everyone made the commitment to participate. We discussed if one of the kids wanted to cancel out of an activity at the last minute, it wasn't fair to the other kids or me. We needed to agree on our activities as a family and all support the group's decision.

This was our official beginning of family meetings.

Every Sunday evening like clockwork, we had our family meeting. We would order or make homemade pizza and discuss the plan for next week over dinner. We used the same guidelines as we used at the dinner table. All ideas were valued and voted on by all of us. We used majority rules as our guide, with me, of course, having the parent power of using a veto when necessary.

My friends would ask, "And they didn't balk at going somewhere ever again?"

Of course they did. They're kids. However, now when they stated they didn't want to go on the family outing at the last minute, I would say, "Remember when we all voted we were going to spend the afternoon roller skating and everyone agreed that was the plan for today? That means we all have a responsibility to carry through with this commitment. You made a commitment to go and I expect you to honor it."

Prior to our family meetings, I would be exhausted trying to talk everyone into going. That changes when you have a commitment from everyone to share in the event.

When someone doesn't want to go, it is then their responsibility to address that feeling and make the best of the situation. Sometimes, I gave them a choice and stated, "You can either come along and bring a book to read, or you can choose to make the best of the situation and see if you can have a good time anyway. Whatever attitude you choose is entirely up to you. However, you do need to honor your agreement in family meeting to attend today."

This meant I didn't give in, but I still gave them some options, some control over their own day. They had permission to feel however they wanted to feel – good, bad or ugly. What I know for sure is that as soon as we arrived at our destination, the child who didn't want to go that day was already eager to begin the activity. They'd get caught up in the excitement and anticipation of what was about to happen. I just saved myself the aggravation of trying to talk them into having a good time.

They learned to accept the responsibility of keeping their word in a commitment.

We added different items to discuss to the family meeting from time to time. One of the things we added: at the beginning of every meeting, each family member had to say something nice that another family member had done for them during the week and how it made them feel. This helped us develop a whole new appreciation for each other.

They all loved the recognition, and naturally, there may have been a little competition to see who could do the most things for the younger two – kind of a nice problem to have.

Everyone's behavior was recognized. We were all learning about being a family and loving each other and respecting each other very early in our family life together.

Sometimes as a mom, I felt like all I was hearing were the complaints, arguments and negative stuff that was happening in the house. The kids would bicker over things and fight, saying mean things to each other. All of which is completely normal. I found a way to balance those moments with saying positive things about each other at family meetings. It was like a family reboot – and it was important to do every week. We all had constant reminders of positive moments. It was a great equalizer and even I looked forward to it every week.

As the children grew older, around middle school age, they weren't all that crazy about attending the family meetings. They felt they were a little too cool for hangin' with the family. Imagine that. However, family meetings became an expectation and therefore attendance was not an option, it was required.

When the grunts and groans began ("Do we have to have another stupid family meeting this week?"), I would respond by reminding them that I valued their input and needed to hear their ideas. If they continued to groan about it, I would teasingly say in my most sincere voice, "Maybe we should just skip it this week and live in utter confusion and chaos, and not hear anyone's ideas about what we're doing this week so none of us will know what's going on. Yes, that's a good idea, Roxie."

Halfway through my sentence, they would begin to smile and know their fight was futile, but they liked the response. Not to be outdone, Mike or Kelly would pipe in with, "Let's give this contestant a '4' for today's performance," (while pretending to hold a scorecard over their head).

I would immediately challenge them, "That was at least a 7!" And the teasing continued as we settled in for the family meeting.

If family meetings sound like a lot of work, picture our family of five eating pizza together once a week for an hour discussing next week's activities. It's very easy when we're all on the same page. It was ten times easier with the family meetings than the chaos that occurs when no one knows what anyone else is doing and all of us are yelling at each other about who's going where, etc. This lesson I learned first hand when we missed a family meeting.

As the children grew older, projects were discussed during family meetings. We all had to agree when the proposed project was taking place so that everyone could help. Projects included raking the yard, washing windows, dry-walling a section of the basement, seal coating the driveway, building railings for the wrap-a-round porch and then painting it, planting and weeding the flowerbeds, shoveling snow off the driveway and sidewalks and washing and cleaning the car, inside and out. Anything we were planning as a family, fun or otherwise, was discussed, as well as what was happening schedule-wise for each person. Everything was marked on the calendar for all to see. We attended everyone's sporting event or school activity as a family, each sitting with friends and socializing so it was a fun time for all. The coordination of schedules helped all of us feel more organized and prepared for the upcoming week.

****

Family meetings are an important way for children to have a voice in weekly activities. The expectation of the family meetings is set by the parent, and part of the child's responsibility as a family member is to provide their input. It is another way for them to feel heard and their ideas and input valued. It also helps them to feel a part of a family team. Positive statements regarding their behavior while interacting with each other during the week made all of us feel good. Weekly family meetings helped us stay connected.

Chapter 19: My Parenting Grade: D–

Report card day at our home was a big deal. When my oldest daughter, Kelly, brought her first grade report card home, it was so great that I twirled her around the room, and we were jumping up and down. She knew I was proud of her when I said, "Let's put your report card on the front of the refrigerator. We can look at it every day and see how great you have done in school every time we walk by the fridge."

At the time, it seemed that was a good idea. Then I heard one of her brothers say he hoped he did that well at school when he got to go. Immediately I tried to place myself in their position. What if they had a learning disorder? How would they feel if their report card was hanging on the fridge for all to see and it wasn't as good as their sibling's?

I learned from his words.

That remark immediately changed the plan for report cards. From that day forward, I learned to sit with each child and talk about grades, school in general, and homework. I listened.

My conversations around grades became geared to how the children themselves felt about the grade. Saying things like, 'I'll always be proud of you regardless of what grade you receive because I know you will be doing your very best." That was the expectation I set for them: that they would do their very best. Telling them, "These are actually your grades, you 'own' them, because you are the one who has done all the hard work to earn the grade so you get to receive all the credit for the grade. I'll just be very, very happy for you."

Asking them how they felt about their grades and just listening became the new plan of action. I never paid them money for their grades as some of their friends' parents did. (And my kids definitely asked for money in the beginning… yep, I would have too if my friend's parents were paying.) Their report card became more of an individual celebration. I think if I had continued to focus on the grades, the children would have become more competitive about their grades. They already placed enough pressure on themselves to be better than their siblings and classmates without me adding to the cause.

It was much more important that the children learn to be proud of their own grades because they earned them. It was about pleasing themselves for their hard work, not their parent. We discussed how each child controlled their own study habits and that each child was therefore responsible for the grade that was earned in each course. They readily accepted the responsibility for their own grades.

Our routine was this: the kids came home from school, had a snack, went out to play and would come in at dinner time. After dinner everyone worked on homework and then we played cards or a game at the kitchen table. They knew they wouldn't be able to play cards if their homework wasn't done. As they grew older, the routine changed to suit their own individual schedule as they all became involved in school activities from middle school through high school.

Earning their own grades was also a way to earn more privileges – the more responsibility they exhibited in doing their best work in school, the more privileges they earned around home and with their friends. The responsibility was rewarded, not the actual report card results.

Staying focused on the positive was a process, however. One day I remember in particular. It was the day of parent-teacher conferences, and I had gone to all four children's conferences. I was booked in teacher meetings all day…two elementary, one middle school with five different teachers and one high school conference with four different teachers. The meetings had gone very well in all areas for all four children.

I was so excited to get home and tell the kids how proud I was to hear all of the compliments the teachers had given each one of them and how much of a leader each of them had become in their respective classes. The teachers stated they were all top-notch students – of course, for me, this was also a celebration internally. This was affirming to me that the kids were doing well in school, building relationships with their friends and earning the respect of their peers, classmates and teachers and giving respect to others in return.

To me, that meant I was succeeding as a single parent. Hooray! Something was working out right. I couldn't wipe the smile off my face. This feeling was short lived.

Walking into the house and seeing that the kitchen was a disaster, I knew a tornado had hit our home. All four children were in the family room watching TV. Storming into the family room, I started yelling, "I can't believe what a mess the kitchen is in! You guys know better than this..."

Then I saw all four sets of eyes staring at me in disbelief! Panic and confusion covered their faces. I took a deep breath and reminded myself to think of the big picture, and realized that this was their day off. They were just hanging out, waiting for me to get home for dinner, and I had suddenly charged in, yelling like a crazed woman.

Stopping abruptly, I said, "I'm going out and will try it again." Walking outside and re-entering the kitchen again, I walked right past the scene of the crime and into the family room.

Excitedly, I exclaimed, "I have the four greatest kids in the whole wide world. Your conferences were fabulous. All of you are doing so awesome that I could hardly fit my fat head into the car to drive home. You must all be so proud of your hard work and terrific grades. I have so much to tell you individually about what your teachers said. I wrote it all down so I wouldn't forget. Then you will be so proud of all your hard work that you'll have the fat head. First I'm going to go upstairs to change clothes, and you may want to check in the kitchen and see if you left anything on the counter. I'll be right down, and we can go out to dinner and talk about your awesome conferences."

Of course, their faces were now smiling and they were suspiciously watching me go upstairs. I said, "What's the matter?"

One of them bravely asked where that other lady went.

I replied, "Oh, the screaming Mimi? She got called away to the desert and she won't be back."

They said, "Do you know how she looked?"

Reluctantly I replied, "Show me" (not really wanting to see what I looked like, but knew this part of the recovery was as good for me as it was for them). Then all four kids took turns doing an imitation of me coming into the family room the first time.

It was hilarious. Of course, they over-exaggerated (they say they didn't), but the end result is that we were all laughing. It was cute to see their sense of humor come into play, because they changed the wording to say, "Now you kids get out in the kitchen and lick every crumb off the table and the kitchen floor...I want it spotless" (in their very gruff voices).

Believe me, those are not my proudest moments, but they are included in the ones I look back on. We all ended up laughing that day and learned something about each other, how to communicate better and to laugh about a mistake and move on as a family. We all knew there were many of those mistakes yet to come. Now we all felt more equipped to handle them.

****

It is important for children to feel proud of themselves for the grades they earn. My job was teaching my children to be responsible for their own actions and to own their behavior. In return, they feel the gratification of that ownership and inner-satisfaction for a job well done. This helps build good self-esteem and helps them to be internally motivated.

Chapter 20: Do Your Parents Know?

Birthday parties – little boys and girls jacked up on sugar – are every parent's nightmare. Kelly had been invited to her friend's second grade birthday party where a single dad was taking his daughter and six of her friends roller-skating to celebrate her birthday. Kelly was excited, as she had never been rolling skating.

Afterwards, I began asking questions (thinking this would be a good idea for our family to have the birthday noise, celebration – and mess – somewhere else besides my own home – clever mom that I am). One of my gazillion questions was, "And did Mr. B. skate the whole time with you kids or did he just watch?"

Kelly quickly answered, "Oh, he just dropped us off and then picked us up when the party was over."

I'm sure I missed the next few minutes of her excitement about the other presents, cake, yada, yada, yada, as my mind was riveted on the dad dropping the kids off and only returning when the party was over. My mind went to: *What would have happened if one of the kids fell and broke her arm?* Now I am not an alarmist parent who takes their kids to the doctor at the first sign of a runny nose or a queasy stomach. Thanks to my years of Emergency Room volunteer experience, my response is the opposite. That ER exposure taught me to remain calm where my best decisions were made trusting my common sense and intuition. The more composed I remained, the more relaxed my children were in any situation or crisis.

But my lesson from this particular birthday party was that all parents don't feel the need to supervise the same way. If I was hosting the party, I would have asked a good friend to go with me and chat for two hours or grabbed a pair of skates and joined the kids circling the rink.

Other parents found out that the girls had just been dropped off at the roller skating rink and they were concerned as well. Calling the parent having the next birthday party and double checking the time of drop off and pick up time, allowed me to gather enough information about the party that I would feel comfortable letting Kelly go.

If it happened to be a skating party (apparently there were other moms who wanted a place to take the jacked-up-sugar-kids and the roller rink seemed to be a popular place), I would volunteer to help carpool the children and stay and skate with them. When I heard, "My husband and I are going to be there the whole time but thanks for offering," from the other parent, I knew I could let my daughter go and just relax and enjoy my time with my other children.

The skating party experience reinforced my own goal that as an involved parent, I would take the time to make the phone call to whomever invited my kids over to play. I had already begun the practice of calling the other parent early on so my children were very familiar with that routine and knew from the beginning that they wouldn't be allowed to go home with anyone after school unless I had talked with the parent before the play date occurred.

Our children need to know that part of caring for children is setting guidelines and safe practices for them to follow.

At elementary age particularly, children need and want those guidelines to feel safe and secure. Beginning the guidelines at such an early age, my children knew the expectations of being an involved parent all the way through high school. (Not that they liked the parent questions in high school, but they were used to the pattern and knew what to expect.)

Quite often as adults, we are all wearing our social masks and no one wants to admit that we are struggling as a parent, so we all give the short answer when asked about how we are doing. "Oh, fine, the kids are great. They sure are keeping me busy."

No one wants to say out loud that we feel like we are floundering and we're not really sure we're doing the right thing for our kids. That would just leave us too vulnerable. Taking parenting classes and investing my time hearing individual speakers helped me to clarify my thoughts and actions regarding my parenting style.

Hearing a speaker at our local high school (when my children were still in elementary school), I tried to prepare myself for what my children would be experiencing in their teen years. The speaker was a parent who talked about wanting her daughter to be popular and quite often let her daughter go and do whatever her friends were doing because all the other parents did. The speaker stressed that her daughter was involved in sports, on high honor roll and had a good relationship with her parents. The mother never suspected her daughter of using drugs so it was a shock when the daughter died from a drug overdose. The audience went silent.

The speaker said if she could change anything in the way that she parented her daughter, it would be this: Love your child enough not to trust him 100 percent. Wow, that was hard to hear.

The speaker stated that teens accept the decisions of peers over parents almost every time so they can be in the in-crowd. Common sense told me she was right; teenage studies proved it. However, I could hardly believe my ears.

She repeated the statement over and over throughout the presentation: Love your child enough not to trust him 100 percent.

The speaker encouraged parents to set up a Parent Support Group where you meet other parents and their children so you feel more comfortable calling another parent that you have previously met and asking them about a party your child has been invited to attend. She emphasized that if we begin this behavior with our children in elementary school and continue it through middle school, it will feel natural to us when our children are in high school. This was already a part of my parenting practice, so this just reinforced that I was doing a good thing for myself and for my children. The more information parents can share, the more our children will have safe boundaries. I will never forget that speaker and her powerful words.

When I began working after the divorce and was first employed at the same school where my children attended, I started Parent Support Groups for parents of students in each of the middle school grades. The Support Group was meant for parents and students to get to know each other and to provide activities and parties that were safe for all attending.

The group began with a night at the school where both parents and students played volleyball together. All students were invited to attend and had to bring at least one of their parents. It was a great way to meet everyone and put names with faces. Usually in elementary school, parents of girls already know a lot of other girl parents from all the birthday/sleepover parties and the same with parents of boys. However, in middle school, parties and activities began to include boy/girl activities and parents didn't know the other gender's parents.

Some nights, parents met without the children present and discussed the Parent Support Group's purpose, which was to provide safe activities and parties for our children and establish open communication among the parents. We were not trying to eliminate parties or diminish our children's fun; we just wanted to have more information and assurance that our kids were safe. We discussed inviting other couples to help chaperone parties so our kids would get used to having adults around.

Our kids resisted the idea of the parent group at first and then discovered they still were allowed to have parties and that made it okay (tolerable). Our kids would get together with their friends and as parents, we knew they would be safe with more adults in attendance. It was very empowering for parents to feel that we had a little more control over where our children were, who they were with and what they would be doing. It enabled parents to enjoy being together, knowing we were all doing the same phone calling and supervision.

At our parent meetings, we discussed what we would do if certain situations occurred. For example, at one of the parent's home, their middle school-aged child had a party and some uninvited high school kids arrived, carrying alcohol under their coats and went immediately to the lower level family room where all the kids were. As parents, we discussed that it was our responsibility to be the bad guy and not allow the older kids to stay. We couldn't expect our children to ask the uninvited kids to leave because our children were caught up in the peer pressure of wanting to be accepted in the popular group. We suggested that an adult approach the uninvited guest(s) and politely, but firmly, ask them to leave. It was the adults' responsibility to remain with the uninvited guests and walk them out the door.

We encouraged parents to give their children the names and phone numbers of other parents who might be able to drive them home if they needed a ride and couldn't reach their own parents.

We encouraged parents to call the host parent and offer to donate pop or snacks for the party; this helped develop good communication among parents. We also stressed that if we received a call from another parent asking questions about an activity at our home, that we should take it as a compliment that our children had friends whose parents care enough to make the call and not be offended that someone was questioning our parenting.

Our group emphasized that we all wanted to make this work so that we could continue phone calls when our kids were in high school. If the majority of the parents of our children's friends participated in the Support Group, the kids would get used to adults coming in and out of the room and could still have fun. We also discussed talking with our children about belonging to the Parent Support Group. Because the kids would talk amongst themselves, they would know that the parents of their friends were also involved in the Parent Support Group.

Our group suggested establishing the rules with our child before having the party, letting them know we would be coming into the party room occasionally and that we would be asking uninvited guests to leave. If your child absolutely refused to accept the guidelines, then the parent would not allow them to host the party. I can guarantee that our children did <u>not</u> want parents to come into the party room. However, this was not negotiable. As parents, it was important for us to be the one establishing the party guidelines. This is another one of those times that parents were not liked by their children.

My kids hated the fact that I was the parent who started the Parent Support Groups every year for eleven years. I validated their feelings. I also made it clear that I was accepting my role as a parent and that meant providing safe guidelines for activities and parties and helping all parents to have open communication. Reminding them that, because I loved them, I wanted the Parent Support Groups to be successful so they could spend more time with their friends.

As my children progressed into high school, I continued to remember the speaker's message: Love your child enough not to trust him 100 percent. What that meant to me was to continue to stay involved with my children. When they wanted to push me away, I found ways to spend time with them one-on-one and keep our communication open. Because I was so involved with each of the Parent Support Groups at the school, parents would tell me where the next parties were and the outcome of the last one. My kids were amazed that I knew information without them telling me, so it was no longer a taboo subject for us to discuss. We put it right on the table.

I actually loved attending all of their school events. Just by showing up and watching them participate told them that I was interested in what they were doing. Sitting with other parents at games and school events was not only fun for me but also gave me information about their circle of friends. A win-win.

Continuing to ask for their help with projects around the house kept us talking while working together. Being involved in household projects also reminded them they were needed and valued as a family member. A family that plays together, stays together and our family always played together.

Why did I tune into the speaker's message? In high school, my friends and I all told our parents that we were going to each other's homes for a sleepover and, of course, never actually spent the night at any of those houses. (I still don't think my parents know, so let's not tell them)… It's fun to share secrets with your friends and keep your parents on the outside. I knew that from my childhood many times over.

Knowing my children wouldn't become my friends until they became an adult and self-sufficient was okay with me. I just needed to be aware of how good those secrets felt for teenagers and try to establish a strong family bond that would help my children to listen to their inner voice and make good decisions when they were with their friends. It also meant that as the parent I needed to listen to my inner voice when something just didn't sound right coming from my teenager.

****

This is one of those difficult times as a single parent when I had to accept my role and the responsibility to set safe guidelines. Sometimes this made me feel very alone. This was also one of the times when I was not very popular with my children. However, I knew that I was strong enough to handle not being liked by my children some of the time. I was doing what was right for them and I was doing what was right for me.

Chapter 21: Allowance and Other Big Bucks

Allowance is a very controversial subject. Are we paying our kids just because they are our kids? That just doesn't make sense to me. Do I get paid to be their mom? Of course not, because I'm sure there would have been many days when the kids would have said, "Sorry, you're fired; we're hiring a better mom than you…a less crabby mom, a better cook mom, a mom with more money to take us places and buy us things, a mom with a snazzy car and not the white station wagon with the fake plastic wood panels on the side." (Which, by the way, they affectionately named 'The Bomb'.)

Many of my friends paid their kids weekly allowances as a way to provide the child with some spending money. The child didn't have to do anything for the allowance. Basically, the parents were paying for the child's spending habits, but now, the child controlled the money. What followed were arguments between parent and child about how the money should be spent.

Raised on an Iowa farm, I grew up helping with family responsibilities. Never having an allowance, the money I earned from babysitting, walking the bean fields and detasseling corn allowed me to choose if I wanted to spend or save it.

In my mind, that was learning about money. My parents taught me that if you didn't have the money in your pocket to buy what you wanted, then you didn't buy it until you earned the money.

I chose to implement a similar system where each child could earn their own spending money. It also taught the kids about budgeting their money.

When it came time for me to answer the children's questions if they could have an allowance because their friend's parents gave them one, I explained it this way: I will be glad to pay you for jobs around the house that I can't accomplish by myself and would have to hire out to someone else. If you are interested in doing the work, you are certainly welcome to do the job for the money.

My children (being the smart kids they are) chose to do the jobs for pay for their spending money. Making a list of all the jobs that needed to be done, I wrote beside each job the amount of money they would earn for that job. They each took turns signing up for jobs. That way the children were proactive in signing up and I stayed out of the bad guy role by having to assign jobs and hear everyone complain that someone else got the good job that they wanted.

If the children didn't have money when they needed it, they learned it was their own fault for not earning it. Sometimes they would ask to borrow money from me, and that's when we negotiated more jobs for pay and the time frame for them to be completed.

As a family member, they also had jobs around the house that they were expected to do because they were a part of the family. They would not be paid for these jobs. For example, each child was assigned helping with the preparation of meals, setting the table and clean-up for one week at a time. It wasn't long before Kelly and Mike took over the cooking of the meal while I was left setting the table, chopping ingredients and supervising. Meanwhile, it was a great conversation exchange about the day's activities and what was happening at school. I was learning more about my children's lives and their friends while we were cooking together.

Each child was also assigned dishes for one entire week at a time. This was the result of listening to them argue night after night about who did the dishes last. The one week of dishes assignment solved the problem.

Sounds easy enough but what about the nights they were at a friend's house working on a school project and wouldn't be home for dinner? It was their responsibility to find a substitute if they were not going to be home for the evening meal. This way, they learned to trade nights with each other, or if no one would trade, they would exchange a favor with me, and I would clean the dishes for them.

It would have been easier to let them get out of dishes, but then I would have always been the one to do the dishes. Plus, the trading of nights with their siblings taught them to negotiate.

Believe me; I am not saying this was easy. Asking kids to negotiate is a tall order. Yes, there were lots of disagreements (actually arguments) over the trading and how fair it really was if no one would trade with them.

And why would no one trade with them? Was it perhaps because they themselves would not trade when they had been repeatedly asked by their siblings? We talked about asking for what you need and asking a second time and stating that you will trade the next time you are asked. I also explained to them how important giving their word becomes in any conversation. Giving your word demands trust. We were all learning to trust each other.

Is this really worth it? Are they really learning anything? At times it seemed more complicated than it was worth. It would have been easier for me just to do the dishes myself and tune out the discussions/arguments; however, that didn't feel right either.

Once again, I learned to trust my inner voice. Finding a way to help them communicate with their siblings and with me and negotiate a result which worked for everyone was not always easy to do. However, with time, the children learned how to accomplish their goal without involving me and still maintain the responsibility for their chores. (Some days seemed very long and sometimes it seemed like they would never catch on. Times four.)

In family meetings, the children set the consequences if the job was not completed or if they failed to get a substitute for their night of dishes. The consequence they selected was to do dishes for the following week so they would have dish detail ("DD" as they liked to call it) for two weeks in a row. One of the kids, not to mention any names (Mike), actually ended up with DD three weeks in a row but learned after that to get substitutes and to do the job right the first time.

Sometimes my children didn't like me for enforcing the rules, but as a parent I had to be strong enough to not want to be their friend all the time. It also meant I had to be able to set the boundary and then remain firm in holding the boundary. Not always easy.

The children were always paid for babysitting their siblings because this was something I felt was not only a necessity for me (to get away for awhile – good self care), it gave them life skills in caring for another person. The guidelines for babysitting meant they would be responsible for playing games with the kids, fixing meals and cleaning up afterwards and being responsible for everyone's safety.

My expectations of the responsibilities were discussed before they made the commitment to me. (Like only one-half hour of TV per day.) It was also a discussion about their responsibility as a role model for their siblings.

"Planting the seed" was not a one-time occasion. Most days I felt like I needed to get a tractor with a field planter and go over and over the same rows because the first seed was lost in the weeds. Eventually, through ongoing discussions, the older children embraced the challenges of being role models and were influencing their siblings in a positive way.

The skills we learn in childhood regarding communication with our own family members and friends help us to be a better co-worker, roommate, spouse, sibling and friend. Good communication helped strengthen my children's confidence and self-esteem. They were leaders in their school classrooms so I knew this was working.

As the children grew older, we discussed chores at our family meetings. We needed to have consequences if the work was not completed by the deadline (which it wasn't; therefore, the need for consequences evolved).

Their responsibility was cleaning two rooms in our home plus their own room by every Saturday at 5 p.m. Seriously, I have seen them with their hair on fire around 4:30 p.m. on Saturdays cleaning their portion of the house. The children set the deadline with my approval and they came up with the consequences. They decided that anyone who didn't complete their part of the cleaning wouldn't be able to go out with friends that weekend or have anyone over during the next week. (I wouldn't have been that strict, but they set the consequences.)

During family meetings, they gave me their word they wouldn't beg me to let them out of the work and still go out with their friends because that wouldn't be fair to me. This actually worked – most days. And yes, they tried the begging and pleading for me to do their work instead (remember, we all have very persistent children).

Reminding them of their agreement that begging me was not fair was mentioned several times (and then some more). By defining my boundaries, I was teaching them how to treat me. Sometimes we were able to work out an agreement; sometimes, we weren't. Focusing on the big picture was the only way I tolerated their reneging. At times it drove me crazy (just a little more than my "ordinary crazy").

At times, I wanted to use Boss-mania mode as it seemed to come to me so naturally. This was all part of everyone learning to have boundaries and keeping the boundaries.

No, I didn't give in.

Yes, I helped them negotiate with either myself or one of their siblings.

Would it have been easier to hire someone to clean our home? Yes.

Could I afford that? No. However, the lessons we all learned through this experience made working through the tough times worth it. Big picture, big picture.

There were times when the Big Picture concept reminded me of a giant TV screen where our lives were being portrayed... At times, it felt like all I was viewing was static.

Giving my children a say in the consequence when they don't keep their agreements helped me in our negotiating process. They're able to better understand the importance of keeping their word than if all the decisions are made by me. If I alone had decided the end result was that they couldn't go out with friends if their work was not completed, the children would have been angry with me.

And yes, they definitely became angry with me when I enforced the rules. However, I'd acknowledge their frustration and ask them if they were more angry with me for enforcing the consequence or more angry with themselves that they didn't complete the task knowing the consequence.

Since they decided what the outcome should be, they realized they were upset with themselves for not doing the work. Of course, they never stated this out loud. And I was strong enough to allow them to be angry with me at the beginning knowing they would realize later on they are really upset at themselves for not completing their responsibilities. This is also the way children learn to set goals for themselves and learn the rewards of accomplishing those goals. Tiny steps, tiny steps.

We all remember the past differently. The children tease me with memories of working their fingers to the bone while their friends were out playing ball or shopping at the mall.

My memories are of music blaring while they were cleaning their portion of the house (a whole 30 minutes before deadline). I've watched them dust a room, then twirl the dust rag into a coil to quickly snap it at the next person walking through the room... and seeing dust particles fly everywhere. Now I won't mention any names here (Mike), however, it does make me smile to remember the little details of just an ordinary cleaning day.

He was probably just trying to make it fun for himself...and isn't that my message to myself...to have fun every day? Hmmmm...maybe the apple doesn't fall far from the tree.

The other thing we learned about getting jobs done around the house was that we accomplished these tasks together as a team. When we all pitched in, we lived in a clean, organized home that we were all proud of.

It was important for us as a family to bond over really good times and fun family events, but also bond together and accomplish tasks of the not-so-fun variety.

****

For me, the most important thing to teach my children about allowances and work around the house was that the best result of a job well done is the feeling of self-accomplishment. The acknowledgement and the money may or may not be there for them in future jobs outside of the home. My children learned to feel good about themselves for their own achievements, to find inner-satisfaction in a job well done. And that feeling promotes good self-esteem.

Chapter 22: May I Borrow Your Staple Gun?

Name one person who wants to ride in a car with four children. I can't think of anyone either. I'll take Acts of Stupidity for $200, Alex. How many times can I say, "Don't make me pull this car over"? Is it wrong of me to want to staple my children's mouths shut?

As a parent, I knew riding in the car would be a challenge and having firm rules for the car right from the beginning certainly helped. Wouldn't you know that car DVD players were not available when my children were young, so we did things the old-fashioned way, and spent the time playing games with each other. These were the rules:

1. The car wasn't started until all seat belts were fastened. No exceptions.
2. Each child was assigned the front seat of the car for one entire month.

There had been so much fighting over the front seat of the car. At first, we tried rotating the front seat position every day. When that failed, we initiated riding in the front seat for one week at a time. Still more quarreling... finally, the assignment of one month at a time. That totally eliminated the front seat fighting. Whew!

If the child whose turn it was to ride in front was not going with us, the front seat was left vacant (otherwise the other three would have bickered over it – tried that, arguing ensued).

This guideline became a blessing because it eliminated the bickering. Yes, peace in the car. Okay I should say, peace *getting into* the car.

Then, I needed my staple gun again.

Remember my goal to have fun every day? Riding in the car with four children made me put that goal into action. I kept a Junior Trivial Pursuit game in the car with just that in mind. The game consisted of flashcards with questions on one side for children aged five to eight, and on the other side questions for nine to 12-year-olds. That game stayed in the car at all times. Sometimes they would beg to bring the game into the house and keep playing, but I was firm that the game always stayed in the car. If I had allowed the game to be brought into the house, they would have grown tired of the game very quickly. It's amazing how something so simple like playing a game in the car can make the car ride much more enjoyable (tolerable).

This too, came with guidelines for the older two children.

First, I talked with Kelly and Mike about playing games that all of us could enjoy. I explained that when we play games and the two younger children guess answers that are incorrect, if Kelly and Mike make fun of their answers (the cruel kind of teasing), then the two younger kids won't want to play the games anymore. Reinforcing the statement that the two younger kids really looked up to their older siblings, I asked both Kelly and Mike what kind of role models they wanted to be. We had had this conversation before... just planting more seeds in role-modeling behavior.

If Kathy or Nick guessed a wrong answer, how would they feel if the bigger kids said they made a good guess at the answer? It didn't take long for the good "guesses" to get compliments from the older kids, and when Kelly and Mike saw how much everyone liked the game, it just made it more fun for all of us. Some of their answers were hilarious.

As the children grew older, Kelly and Mike shared a kids' car for summer work purposes, and their schedule made it very clear that they had to communicate. When Kelly and Mike were in high school, they were both employed at the local country club, where Kelly worked as a waitress and Mike was part of the grounds crew. Mike would have to go to work at 5:30 a.m., so he would get Kelly out of bed to drive him to work so she could use the car to drive to work at 10 a.m. for the lunch shift. Mike would then bring the car home at 3 p.m., and she would call him for a ride home around midnight when her shift was over.

They shared the car for work and I never heard them complain about driving each other around to work or getting out of bed, whether it was early morning or late at night to pick up or drop off their sibling.

The rest of the stuff I heard them argue about – like who was hogging the kids' phone line (before cell phones) or who had the car last for a night out with their friends, etc. was an ongoing discussion with them which I figured was pretty normal. (Maybe it wouldn't hurt to invest in the heavy duty staple gun, just in case...)

Prior to Kelly leaving for college, I was constantly working on the competitive nature between Kelly and Mike. They were always trying to outdo the other one, regardless of the task. Sometimes the competition was good, sometimes it wasn't. Most times it drove me crazy. The competition between them lasted all the way through high school. When Kelly left for college, they still had a shaky relationship. It made me very sad to think I failed at trying to help them become best friends.

Another surprise.

While Kelly and I talked on the phone several times a week after she left for college, it was only a few weeks of her being away that she began calling home and talking with Mike. Their phone calls lasted 30-45 minutes a couple of times each week. Now that she was away from home, they had figured out they really missed each other, and those late night phone calls – on the very phone they argued over – started the beginning of their lasting friendship. Go figure.

****

Setting guidelines for the children's behavior in the car and helping them to find ways to entertain themselves proved to be the solution for fun, memorable car trips together.

Chapter 23: Testing the Boundaries – Again and Again and Again

Testing their boundaries when my kids were teenagers was probably the most frustrating thing I had to endure, and I'm sure it was equally frustrating for them. Now that my children are over that stage, I can appreciate it much more. When they were going through the boundary-testing, I was certain there were times that all of the love, fun and laughter between us was gone, based on the way they were acting. There were so many times at night when I would go to bed and feel sad and confused, thinking I was now failing at this parenting job after working hard for so many years.

Was all the work for nothing? Have I lost them for good? Then a day or two later, things would get talked through and we would end up negotiating a solution and would be on the same page again. Listening to their feelings and their suggestions on how to resolve the situation helped us to reconnect. I never wanted to give up trying to stay connected with them.

During the teenage years I learned my children didn't always like me because I was strong enough to do the right thing and make them accountable for their actions. I wasn't always their friend, but I was always their parent.

Here's an example: my oldest son, Mike, and a group of his friends were playing baseball at the city park and one of Mike's coaches called to change the time of his team's baseball practice. Before the age of cell phones, I drove to the park to tell Mike his practice time was changed, and as I was walking up to the group of boys who had not seen me approach, I could hear lots of swearing, laughter and "smack talk" among the group. It wasn't a surprise to hear this kind of language.

Mike was given his message and then I asked all the boys to gather around. I began by stating that I heard their language as I approached the group. Mike was cringing and the look on his face said, "Don't start lecturing my friends."

Remaining calm, I asked the boys to look over to the side of the park where a father was coaching soccer to a group of 9 and 10-year-old girls. They heard the same language that I had heard. Next, I informed them it was not fair to force these girls to listen to the swearing because the park is a public place.

Then I heard "Sorry," "Sorry," and "We won't swear anymore" from the group of boys, while my son, Mike, was hanging his head, feeling mortified that his mother had just reprimanded his entire group of friends. How humiliating for him.

Walking off the field, I went over to where the father was practicing soccer with his team. I apologized for my son and his friends and the language they were using and informed him that I had talked with the boys about it. The father was very appreciative.

However, I felt a huge knot in my stomach while walking to my car, knowing Mike was probably hating me for the embarrassment I had caused him.

When Mike arrived home from the park, he surprised me by apologizing for the bad language and stated that only he and one of his friends were responsible for the swearing and that the other boys in the group were not participants in the profanity. Acknowledging his courage in taking responsibility for his actions, I asked him to call the soccer dad, who we knew through our church, and apologize for his swearing at the park.

He refused. He said he couldn't do it because he wouldn't know what to say. I didn't accept his answer and suggested he write down what he wanted to say and when he was speaking to the dad, he could read from his notes.

This was another time when my kids didn't like me (probably hated my guts – I'm sure Mike did at that moment – I would've too if I was the kid). He had come to me and apologized for his swearing and in his mind, that should have been enough. I wanted Mike to own his behavior and apologize for it, rather than having his mom do it for him.

Mike was truly unhappy with me, to put it mildly. I never raised my voice, but once again, I took a deep breath and stated my expectations of him. I asked him to make the phone call before he went to bed that evening. The sooner we face something, the less anxiety we have around it.

Even though I was very calm in my request to him, doubt swirled inside my head the whole time. *What if this hurts our relationship and he doesn't want to laugh and joke around anymore? What if he doesn't want to have his friends over now that I have reprimanded all of them?* And, in the back of my mind, *What do I do if he doesn't make the phone call?*

I knew I was doing the right thing but it certainly didn't feel good putting it into action. Mike spent the majority of the evening in his room and I was feeling worse by the minute. Finally, just before I was getting ready to go to bed, Mike came to me and said he had called the soccer dad and apologized and that the dad was really nice on the phone and thanked him for his phone call. I hugged Mike and told him I was proud he had the courage to call and own his behavior and that I hoped he was proud of himself as well.

That week in church, the soccer dad thanked me for Mike's phone call. I needed that thank you.

One of the reasons that parenting is so hard is that this scenario happened over and over again.

Once the children were grown and through this stage, I realized that they were experimenting with their feelings and the guidelines, and trying to set their own boundaries. I also realized that the best time for them to rebel was when they are still at home, with parents around and available, and not out on their own where no one is there to reel them in when they overextend themselves.

Little by little I accepted this rebellion and tried to understand my role of being there to negotiate and not just watch from afar, or worse, not know about it at all. Learning to work through problems together as a family, we were making everyone stronger and more committed to each other —maybe not right away, but in the days ahead. It was a learning curve for all of us.

As a single parent, I had to set the boundary and hold the boundary while experiencing resistance from my child. It was during these moments that I desperately wanted to have a mate who would talk it through with me and assure me this was the right thing to do. Or help me find a better solution for the issue at hand. Or be the mediator between the child and me.

But in reality, I didn't have a mate. Those were the times that I felt very alone. *Am I being too strict? Has everything I've done gone down the drain?* I tried to stay grounded and be consistent. Some days I fell short.

Sometimes my life felt like the movie "Groundhog Day" (coincidentally, the movie was filmed in our hometown). My days seemed like a constant repeat of testing the boundaries with all four children. If only I could have invented a breakfast cereal, fortified with patience, love and fairness for all, I would have devoured it every morning just to get me through each day.

****

When you set healthy boundaries for yourself, you increase your own self esteem. You are teaching your children how to treat you. When you acknowledge their boundaries, you are increasing their self-esteem.

Chapter 24: Big Brother Talks

Being on a very frugal budget, I became a very discerning buyer of clothes and necessities. I never wanted to create the image to the children that we were poor, but the truth is, we were poor. Even with child support checks, our family qualified for the reduced lunch program at school. Being too proud to apply for the reduced lunches, I wanted to prove to myself that we could make it without financial help. Maybe some other family needed help more than we did.

Clothes shopping presented a challenge for me. Resale shops became second nature. Hand-me-downs were shared from other families. My kids grew up accepting this because they didn't know anything different.

One thing I always did was to purchase a popular brand name of sneakers for each child when they reached middle school so they would feel like they fit in with their peers. The children also had earned their own spending money, and when it was time to go school shoe-shopping, the deal went down like this: I would pay for their regular pair of sneakers for school and it could be any brand that the child would pick. They would be responsible for purchasing any other sneakers they wanted or needed. In middle school, the kids were required by the school to take a different pair of gym shoes for their gym locker and keep those sneakers at school all year. (They could then be worn in gym class when the child wore sandals or dress shoes to school.)

Since I was working at the school, I learned very quickly that students forget to lock their gym lockers and their gym shoes get lost... a lot. My request was that my kids purchase an inexpensive pair of gym shoes with their own money, knowing they would take better care of their gym shoes that they purchased themselves (and lock their gym lockers). Maybe they wouldn't lose them as easily if they knew they had to replace the lost ones with their own pocket money.

This brings us to the shoe-buying incident.

Nick was in sixth grade and we were school shopping for sneakers. The kids were all trying on shoes in their size, and I was going back and forth between the aisles when I saw that Nick was trying on Nike shoes for his gym shoe purchase.

Step in, Mrs. Shoe Authority. I told him that since he already had one pair of Nike shoes for his regular school shoes, he should probably buy an inexpensive pair for his gym shoes. Babbling on, I told him that he might outgrow the shoes in the middle of the year and he would be wasting his hard earned money on expensive Nike gym shoes, blah, blah, blah. That was my rationalization for wanting him to buy the cheap shoes for gym. I was doing a very good job of trying to talk him into seeing things my way, or so I thought.

However, the sad look on his face told me that he was not happy with this information. Letting him think about it, I said I'd check on the other kids and come back to him. Walking to the very next aisle over in the shoe department, the boys did not know I was close enough to hear their next conversation.

Mike, an eighth grader, came over to Nick and said, "What's the matter?" Clearly he noticed the long face as well.

Nick replied, "Mom said I couldn't buy these Nike sneakers for gym, but I think if I'm spending my own money, I should be able to buy whatever shoes I want. And I want these."

Mike asked, "Did you tell mom that?"

Nick said, "No."

Mike paused for a moment, as I eagerly waited to hear his next words. Finally, he said, "Well, it's the hardest thing you're ever going to have to do, but you've just got to go up against her."

What? Go up against her? The hardest thing you're EVER going to have to do? That statement alone made me feel like Godzilla in the next aisle – I felt like a huge scary beast that people run from – I honestly didn't know whether to laugh or cry.

Mike continued, "You tell Mom that it's your money, you earned it, and you think you should be able to spend it the way you want to. And you want to buy these shoes. Do it, Nick. I'll be right here."

111

I stood frozen in the next aisle. Part of me wanted to run over there and tell them I heard everything and buy him the shoes because I didn't think of myself as this big ogre that "you just have to go up against."

Part of me wanted to laugh out loud at the description that I had heard and the mental picture that formed in my mind.

But mostly, I just wanted to go over and hug Mike for giving his little brother the encouragement and words he needed to hear to start those steps into his manhood. Speak up for yourself – wasn't that the message I had preached to them all along, trying to help them voice their opinions?

And then I knew what I needed to do.

I needed to let him "go up against me" so that he would have the courage to speak his mind the next time, and the time after that. Rounding the corner of the aisle and feeling grateful that I was standing close enough to hear this exchange, I saw Nick waiting to talk with me.

Asking him if he had decided what he wanted to do, I saw my child with these incredibly big brown eyes looking up at me. He probably had to muster every ounce of courage he had to speak his mind. Knowing if I listened hard enough, his pounding heart could be heard as he said, "I think since I worked for this money and it's my money, I should be allowed to buy whatever I want with my own money." His voice was a little shaky starting out and grew stronger as he spoke, "And I want to buy these shoes."

There it was. He said it.

Standing silent for a while, as if thinking it over, I finally said, "You know, you're absolutely right. It is your money, and you're the one who worked for it, and you should be allowed to spend it the way you want. Good point. So let's do that. You buy those for gym shoes, and I'll buy your school shoes." And then I walked away.

I was almost running to the next aisle because I couldn't wait to hear the next conversation between the boys. Mike said, "See, I told you that you could do it and now you get to buy your shoes."

As for Nick, I pictured the biggest grin on his face that would last all day.

And for me, the lesson just learned by hearing their conversations was how important it was for me to listen to my children and hear their needs. Now, I knew right from the beginning of this whole incident that Nick would outgrow his two pairs of Nike sneakers in a very short time. We would be out shopping for new shoes again very soon. However, I also knew if I took away his right to speak his mind and be heard, it would be even more destructive in the long run. He had to learn some of these life lessons by trying out his own decisions.

Allowing my children to fail, even when I knew better, was harder than I imagined.

Later that night when I was saying goodnight to him, I asked if he was proud of himself for speaking his mind about buying the shoes that he wanted with his own money. His eyes sparkled and I could almost feel his self-confidence growing as we spoke. Sharing with him that I could see he was proud of himself as well, because speaking out to a parent is a very difficult thing to do, made him smile all the more. I assured him how impressed I was that he was brave and very respectful in speaking his mind.

And then I received one of the biggest hugs as we both shared in his victory.

I, too, went to sleep that night with the same huge smile on my face. Even ogres smile when they're happy.

****

This "incident" told me a lot about our family of five. It told me that Mike had already learned to speak up to me as a parent, a difficult and brave thing to do as a child, and now he was passing that experience on to his brother. Mike modeled the behavior that I had encouraged the older two children to do for their younger siblings and it was working, right in front of me. Mike gave Nick the words to use and stated he would be right there with him when he spoke up to me and then he stepped aside and let Nick do the work. When I saw the role modeling and the "speaking up for yourself "working in my children, I knew the work I was doing as a parent was effective, which made me feel proud and encouraged me to stay connected to my children. My message: just keep listening.

Chapter 25: The Sex Talks

Great! Just what we all want our kids to know...more information about sex. *And who tells them and at what age? Me? Yikes! How will I know what to say?*

Thinking about my years growing up and what information my parents gave me about sex is where the task began. That took about ten seconds because my parents never told me anything directly. There were statements such as "nice girls don't park" and "nice girls don't get into trouble" (this meant pregnant, even though we never really said the word out loud, we all knew what "trouble" meant). Phrases such as, "nice girls don't go to drive-in movies" and "nice girls don't drink or smoke" were my guidelines.

I can remember driving into our farmyard coming home with a date and the yard light immediately went on, and not because of a motion detector device. It was because my mother was up waiting for me to come home. If we stayed in the car and talked, (and I seriously mean talk here, as in exchanging words back and forth), after five minutes, the yard light would flash off and on several times. That was the signal to come into the house because, of course, nice girls don't park.

So, naturally, parking was intriguing to me, because it was so forbidden. Usually we parked along some country road, which was really much more dangerous because our car lights were out, and we could have been hit by another car driving on the road. Apparently, nice girls sometimes rebel.

All I remember is feeling guilty when I did park on a date. Who doesn't enjoy kissing and being held in someone's arms? I loved all of that. This is not to blame my parents as they did what they thought was right. This reflection just helped me to know that I wanted more communication on this subject with my own children.

As the parent, I wondered, *"What are the goals I want to accomplish in giving my children information about sex and sexuality?"* I know I'm a good girl but when I was growing up, I felt like a bad girl because I had broken the good girl rules. I wanted my children to grow up to be comfortable with lots of hugs and kisses and being told they are loved, not only by me but by others as well.

Through counseling, I learned that I am worthy of loving myself. I wanted that same feeling for my children. When you feel you are loved and believe you are worthy of loving yourself, you have the ability to give love to others. If we know we are loved and admired for who we are, we don't need to look to someone else to try to make us feel loved. When we learn to love ourselves, the love from others is very inviting and authentic. When we are incapable of feeling love from within, we become needy and look to others to make us happy and make us feel loved. Everything I had read stated that, as a parent, I would know when to openly discuss sex with my younger children because they would begin to ask questions.

When I was eight months pregnant with my fourth child, we were sitting at the dinner table one night, and Kelly, who was seven at the time, asked, "So when you eat your dinner, does the food just go plop, plop, plop on top of the baby's head and that's how the baby gets food in your stomach?"

She continued, "What if the food lands on the back of the baby's head? How does the baby get it into its mouth?"

This is what the book was talking about. The children begin to ask questions, and you give them answers to satisfy their interest. Right?

Before I could answer, she continued, "And how does the baby even get inside your stomach in the first place? Do you swallow her when she is little and then she just keeps eating and getting bigger inside of you?"

I wanted to burst out laughing. "Those are excellent questions, and you and I will talk about the answers later when you're taking your bath." Immediately changing the subject to something different, she seemed pacified for the moment.

This had given me time to think about what I wanted to convey to my seven year old daughter, and while she was enjoying her bath, our conservation went like this:

"You asked me about how the baby gets into my tummy, and I would like to explain how that happens. When parents love each other, they talk about having children together and our bodies were created to fit together while we are making love. Just as it feels good to have a back rub and to be hugged and touched, it feels good to hug and lay close to someone you love. The man's body produces a seed which is given to the woman's body and begins to grow in the woman's body in a very special place called the womb which sounds like 'room' only with a 'w'. That special womb in a woman's body is where all babies grow. It's right next to a woman's tummy so the food the mommy eats goes into her tummy and is separate from the womb. The baby is connected to the mommy by a cord and is fed through the cord just the amount that the baby needs as it begins to grow."

Thinking I had calmly explained this to my seven year old daughter surprised me a little. But then she asked, "So how does the seed get into your womb? (And hearing a seven year old say 'womb' made me want to laugh out loud because she said it so precisely and intentionally.) Do you swallow the seed?" (Again, trying not to laugh.)

Just when I thought I was done explaining, she's asking for more.

Calmly, I took a deep breath and stated, "Well, you already know that men have a penis and women have a vagina and that's how our bodies are different and when we're making love, a man's penis fits into the woman's vagina and the seed is placed in the woman's body while they are making love."

Whew! I explained how the whole baby thing worked with all the correct terms. We had already been using the correct terminology for our body parts so the words penis and vagina were already known to her. My daughter looked very comfortable with this information so I was feeling pretty darn good.

It was then Kelly calmly stated, "I'm glad that you waited until my bath time because I think if I'd heard that at dinner, I might have thrown up." I didn't know whether to laugh or cry. So much for my awesome explanation.

I apologized for making her feel sick and assured her that she would understand as she grew older and promised her that it would not make her sick (which I knew would be a whole different conversation a few years down the road).

Our usual routine at bedtime was brushing teeth, a story in bed or sometimes a quick backrub and a discussion of the day's events. This turned out to be a wonderful routine because as the kids got older, this was the down time of the day. Since the lights were out in the bedroom, it was a good way to discuss things as they were getting their backrub.

Somewhere between first and second grades with each of the children, we talked about our bodies being very special because they are our bodies and they belong to us. Explaining that each of our bodies was created just as they are meant to be, our job was to take good care of our bodies. We are in charge of eating good foods to help us grow taller and stronger and by playing outside and exercising our bodies, we develop healthy habits.

Then I would add, "Your private parts are also important for you to take good care of."

And I made sure they understood that we don't have to share our private parts with anyone and if anyone asks you to touch his/her private parts or wants to touch your private parts, that person is wrong. Encouraging the children to come and tell me or tell another adult was the message and assuring them that I will make certain they don't have to be around that person again. Ever!

Talking with the girls about sex over the years was much easier, partly because they asked questions and were open to discussions.

It was more difficult for me with the boys. The Sex Talk with each of boys occurred separately around junior high age; I chose to keep it simple and made it funny.

Deciding to write out a script to read to them separately made it fun for me to think about and put together.

"Instead of our usual chit-chat," I began, "tonight we're going to have a sex talk." Before they could even respond, I quickly continued, "Now you don't have to say a thing, as I have written out a script for us to use when we have our official sex talk and this will be a practice session tonight."

By now they think I'm completely crazy, and they're in shock that I am discussing this out of the blue as they are in the mode of independence and the last thing they need is sex information from their mom.

"Here's how this will work. I'll read through the script tonight out loud and you don't have to say anything and then you can think about it for a couple of days, and we can rehearse it another night," (which we never did, as I meant for the script to be a method of getting the information on the table). I begin reading both parts out loud.

"Mom: How about a good old fashioned sex talk for tonight's conversation?

Son: That's a good idea.

Mom: O.K., here's the scoop. In your health class, you'll be learning all about the human body and how men and women's bodies are different. Let's begin with the woman's body."

This is where I would start discussing menstruation in girls growing into women's bodies and how nature begins this process as early as fifth grade for some girls and later for others.

"Son: So, Mom, why is it important for me to learn about girls' bodies?

Mom: "Well, it's important because in any relationships you have with women, you'll have better communication and understanding of them if you know how their bodies work."

As I'm reading all of this, I know my son is probably thinking, geeeeez, I have a math test tomorrow and here my mom is, in my room, yapping on and on about this stupid sex talk thing and I just want her to zip it and get out of my room. However, there's also a part of him that curiously wants to know more. I continue reading from the script.

"Mom: Remember when you were little and we talked about our private parts and how we respect the private parts of ourselves and others? This is important when you begin dating a girl. You will teach her how to treat you, and she will teach you how you can treat

119

her. That is what respect is all about. How would she feel about you if your actions said that you didn't have respect for your own body or for hers? Are your actions ones that make you proud of who you are? Those are all questions that only you can answer. And if you are doing some touching that a girl doesn't want, then you are not being respectful of her.

Son: Man, this sounds like very important stuff. And serious stuff, too.

Mom: Relationships can be very fun and yet some can be very complicated. You always need to know that you have a say in what the outcome will be by the decisions you continue to make in that relationship. By not making any decisions, you are choosing to allow the other person to make all the decisions for you. By making all the decisions yourself, you are disrespecting the other person's right to have a say in the relationship. I know you are good at listening to others and that's important in getting along in any relationship so you are ahead of the game in that regard. Our family often talks about compromising and negotiating and those are important skills to take into the relationships you'll have with both boys and girls. Remember when we talked about how our actions and our words define our reputation? That's all part of treating ourselves and others with respect."

I continued to read, "Well, that's all I have in the script so far, but next week, I'll have written the discussions we'll have about oral sex and venereal disease.

Son: I can't wait."

Neither of my sons talked during this entire time except to laugh out loud where I was reading his lines about how interested he was and asked for more information, furthered by statements from him like "Oh, yeah, that's something I'd definitely say.... NOT." But the bottom line is: they listened.

For me, this was an easy avenue into leaving brochures on their dressers regarding sexual information when they were in high school. I added a handwritten note which said that they should study the pamphlet as I had a quiz for them to take. It was my way of giving them the information and adding a little humor so it didn't seem so secretive and forbidden.

Not to be outdone, shortly after finding the brochure, they'd announce to me they were ready to ace the quiz, all said with that smirk that says "Don't mess with me, Mom, 'cause you can't tell me anything I don't know" kind of look.

Periodically, I would mail them brochures with a cover letter that stated it was specifically for them, signed by Venus, the Love Goddess. Their comments of wishing to receive money instead of brochures made me smile, but I did notice that the brochures ended up in their rooms and not in the garbage.

Another time when one of my sons was in high school and dating a girl quite seriously, I asked if we could have a discussion about their relationship. It ended up being a one-way conversation coming from me with the intent of offering some things for him to think about.

Beginning with the statement that he was old enough to make his own decisions, I also stated that by having this conversation, I wasn't trying to sway his decisions nor did I expect him to answer any questions during this conversation. These were merely suggestions for him to think about on his own and answer the questions only to himself.

My son was 18 at the time and a senior in high school. I was positive that he didn't want to listen to anything I had to say, but I felt it was my responsibility as a parent to have this discussion.

Beginning the conversation, I started with the facts as I knew them. Stating he was having a serious relationship with Kerrie (not her real name) and when relationships get serious, sometimes they also include sexual intercourse. Acknowledging a loving sexual relationship can be a very important and beautiful part of a marriage or monogamous relationship, it can also be a very healthy, enjoyable part of a committed relationship. I stated I knew he was interested in applying to colleges and going away to school the following year, and was wondering what decisions he would make if Kerrie got pregnant. Seeing him tense a little, I knew I had made him uncomfortable with my brazen comment. I went on to say, there

121

are lots of couples who get pregnant and weren't planning on it. It just means there will be some changes in plans.

Thinking about this for long time, I had written down my questions for him. Remaining calm in my approach, I began by reminding him that he didn't have to answer out loud.

1. What would happen if she didn't want to keep the baby? Would you support that decision?
2. What if she wanted to keep the baby and get married?
3. Would you finish high school and where would you want to live?
4. Would this change your decision about going to college?

He definitely did not want to talk about this. It was uncomfortable for him as his body language was tense and his scowling facial expression told me that he wanted this conversation to end. It wasn't pleasant for me knowing that I was making him uneasy; however, I reminded myself many times that it was my responsibility as a parent to have this discussion whether he was comfortable or not.

Apologizing for making him uncomfortable and stating it was part of the responsibility of being a good parent to have these discussions, I thanked him for listening. Acknowledging that one day when he had a family, I knew this memory would come back to him and he would have the courage to reach out to his children because he would love them and take his responsibility of being a good parent very seriously.

Then I hoped that I had done the right thing.

****

Conversations about sex and intimacy are important discussions to have with your children even if they are uncomfortable for parent and/or child in the beginning. Then the topics do not seem off-limits or unspeakable as time goes on. The goal is to create a safe place for your children to discuss their feelings. For me, humor was my weapon of choice.

Chapter 26: The Silver Lining

Listening. Why is that so difficult? Reminding myself over and over again to listen became the norm for me because most days were just too hectic to do it naturally. So many times when the kids were telling me something that had happened to them, or a friend was hurting and telling me their story, I wanted to rush into the conversation and fix it with my suggestions and ideas. However, I didn't like it when someone interjected their solutions to my problems.

Most of the time, I want to resolve my own problems and I just need someone to listen to me, to let me talk it out.

However, there are times when a different perspective is warranted and the key is to know when those opportunities occur.

One such occasion presented itself when my son, Mike, was a freshman in high school and came home late after football practice. Looking at his face, I knew he was upset.

"It looks like you had a tough practice," I said, continuing to fix dinner.

Mike sat down at the kitchen table and began his story, "You won't believe what happened to me today. First, in math class, there was a whole bunch of us standing around talking when the bell rang. Mr. T said that we were supposed to be in our seats ready for class and since we weren't, he sent me to the dean's office. Me, the only one who got sent to the office when there must have been eight or nine of us standing there talking. It's so unfair that I was the only one sent."

His voice sounded more frustrated as he continued, "Then Mr. B (the dean) said I had a detention after school today but instead of going to the detention room, I had to go to his office and he gave me a garbage bag. He told me to go out to the parking lot and pick up garbage for the whole detention. Everyone else who had detentions gets to work on their homework but I had to pick up garbage outside. It was so disgusting. After all that, it made me late for football practice. You know the coach hates it when anyone is late. He made me stay after practice and run hills for another 30 minutes and kept yelling at me the whole time. This was the worst day ever." By this time, he was angry and frustrated and practically shouting.

Sitting down with him at the table, I took a deep breath and said, "It sounds like it was a rotten day and I don't blame you for being upset."

After a pause, I added, "However, I do have to tell you that it sounds like your teachers all count on you as a leader." Mike looked at me as if I hadn't heard his story at all and was perplexed as to how I came up with that absurd response. (I was used to that look.)

Immediately, I continued, "When a teacher is going to send someone to the office, they certainly aren't going to send eight or nine kids, because it would mean the teacher doesn't have his class under control. The teacher only needs to send one student, the leader of the group, to the office to get his message across to the other students. If he sends the leader, the others in the group realize how lucky they are that they didn't have to report to the dean's office and that leader will probably take his seat before the bell rings next class period. Naturally, the other kids will follow his lead."

Continuing, I added, "The Dean usually knows the student body fairly well and he already knew that you were a leader in your class by your academic standing and your leadership award from middle school. The dean knows you will get your homework done and could trust you to go outside and pick up trash. Other students receiving detentions require supervision. You, as a leader, don't need supervision. Crummy job that you had to do, but I certainly can understand why he chose you to do it, because you're trustworthy."

Now I had his attention, "And then, your football coach: you are one of the captains of the team and he expects you to set the example for the rest of the players. He's counting on you to be a leader in the classroom, as well as on the field, so that's why you got yelled at and had to run hills. I'm sorry to hear that you had such a rotten day but I'm proud of the fact that your teachers and coach know you are a leader. It's not always easy being a leader, but you can turn this around. I sure wouldn't have wanted to be the player who lined up across from you in scrimmage today because I'm sure that kid took a beating."

We both smiled a little, knowing that poor kid probably got the brunt of Mike's frustration. Mike and I both knew that a good way to discharge anger is to physically release it through exercise as we had discussed this before in our family. I could tell by the end of our conversation that Mike understood what I was saying as he was already exhibiting the requirements of being a leader.

His facial expression had relaxed and his next words were, "Let's eat. I'm hungry."

I knew we were back on track.

I have thought about this conversation with Mike many times. Working at the school, I've heard many parents' reactions to their children having detentions or getting into trouble with teachers at school. Hearing their remarks helped me to figure out how I wanted to handle my own children when they were in trouble. Here are some of the other potential reactions and results:

1. Criticizing the behavior of the child for getting into trouble and making him/her feel even worse. "I can't believe you weren't in your seat when the bell went off. No wonder you were sent to the dean's office." This reaction made the child feel as if they were being punished twice. The child learned not to share anything else with his parent.

2. Taking the child's side and berating the teacher for yelling at their child. "That's totally unfair; your teacher never should have done that." This action pits child against teacher and builds a barrier between the two and isn't conducive to a healthy learning relationship.

3. Making the situation about the parent or blowing it out of proportion, i.e., "Why are they picking on my kid? I'm going to call that teacher and tell them that they are not going to pick on you again. I'll call the dean or the superintendent if

I have to." Now the child doesn't want to tell the parent anything because he's afraid that he'll be in even more trouble at school. More importantly, he has lost the trust that it is safe to tell his parents what goes on at school.

4. Dismissing the child's frustration because the parent is so wrapped up in their own problems. "I can't even think about your problem right now because my day was even worse," or "Just forget about it, it's over now," which makes the child feel unimportant and invisible.

At the end of the day, I knew that I had validated Mike's feelings that he had a rotten day. Feeling grateful that I was able to help him look at his day from another perspective made me feel better too. It reinforced one of my goals of providing a safe place for him to share his feelings. Another baby step in the right direction.

****

As a parent, stepping back and looking at the big picture can help diffuse a situation. Remaining calm and listening to their entire story helps you to reframe it for your child. Because I was very conscious of the negative messages from others that I allowed into my head, I was constantly working on putting positive messages on the "video tape" in my children's heads. My goal was to help them create a healthy self-esteem and a strong mental image of themselves.

Chapter 27: What? Another Project?

Some days I hated all the work. *Where is that magic wand when I need it? Who took my copy of "Single Parenting for Dummies?" Surely there's a chapter on how to make all the kids do the work while I go shopping.*

Over time our family learned to do projects together, mainly because I couldn't afford to hire a professional to do it. Our reward was a feeling of accomplishment and teamwork within the family, and that became the biggest gift of all in doing these projects. Yes, I certainly saved money, and the kids always had a choice if they didn't want to tackle the project, but the important lesson was that we learned to fix so many things on our own and worked together as a team.

The added bonus was that it gave us wonderful stories to tell later on from both viewpoints: theirs, and the correct version…which, of course, would be mine. When I begin to reminisce about how much fun we had working together, they say, in perfect mockery, "If we all work together, it'll only take 15 minutes." Allegedly, I described a job as taking 15 minutes if we all worked together, and the job actually took much longer. The phrase was then attached to every job going forward (by them) whether it was 15 minutes or 4 hours. For the record, I may have mentioned it might take 15 minutes or so a few times, but who's counting?

Every fall and every spring, the kids and I would have to rake the leaves, and this in itself seemed to be a monumental task. The leaf-raking seemed like the easiest part – getting the kids to agree on the day and the time was the challenge. This was discussed at family meeting time so we all agreed on what worked best for each of our schedules. It was very important to have everyone on the same page and allow everyone to have input on the time and day of our chore, because otherwise it would have turned into an argument (she said from experience).

The kids love telling the yard raking story. At first we started by raking leaves into piles and while raking, we tried to make it fun by asking each other questions. Everyone took turns answering. What was your favorite birthday present and why? Whose birthday party of your friends was the most fun? What's your favorite ride at Six Flags? And so on. One conversation led to the next. Their stories were hilarious.

They always argued over who got to help me pick up the big piles of leaves in black garage bags. Usually Kathy, the youngest of my children, held the bag while I picked up the leaves and dumped them into the bag. You guessed it: whoever was chosen or volunteered to pick up the leaves with me, the other kids complained that they had the easiest job and why didn't I pick them to do the bagging job? *Come on, seriously…who cares? I can't believe we're arguing over this.*

To settle this repeated argument, I offered a suggestion: all of us would rake the leaves. Then we would all pile the leaves on a big king size bed sheet and carry it to the curb with each of them holding one corner of the sheet. I thought this would solve the problem, making all four parts exactly the same. Usually the boys would then empty the bed sheet onto a huge pile of leaves on the curbside for the city to pick up with their enormous leaf sucker-upper machine.

The kids soon added this rule: as soon as the bed sheet was emptied of all the leaves, the last person who touched it had to drag it to the back yard for the next load. Now we all know that the bed sheet wasn't heavy when it was empty but, for some unknown reason, no one wanted to carry it back. The last person that had it would roll it in a ball and throw it at another person and whoever it touched last had to carry it to the backyard. So it became a "throw the leaves on the huge pile by the curb and run for your life to the backyard without getting hit by the wet, smelly, bed sheet game."

We must have had 10 - 12 loads of leaves each season, and it still made us laugh to run every time so we wouldn't get caught carrying back the bed sheet. Being the supervisor of this event was a wise decision for me, mainly because I would have been whacked in the head with the wet, smelly bed sheet every time. I was, in fact, the weakest link in this running game.

The smack talk actually started as they were carrying the sheet down to the curb. The anticipation of who was going to get hit by the disgusting thing kept our adrenaline going. It was a silly game, but it made all of us have fun doing the work together, and we didn't dread the bi-annual leaf-raking, wet, smelly bed sheet job... too much.

****

Creating teamwork in a family can seem like herding cats on some (or most) days. Patience and flexibility add to the strength of a good leader. When every team member shares in the work or the play, each person feels connected. Strong, positive teamwork builds self-esteem.

Chapter 28: The Attitude Drawer

This brings me to another one of my favorite stories. Nick was in high school, and while the other kids fought verbally with each other for the bathroom, phone time, use of the kid's car, (i.e., everything), Nick, my third child, was quieter. He'd always been the most reserved of all the children. He never asked for much and was one of the hardest workers I'd ever seen. However, around the age of 15 or so, his moods began to change. He became crabbier in the morning and just didn't speak to anyone. The expression on his face made us very aware that no one should ask him anything.

How does someone change this? Can they? This wasn't the way he had been acting all the time growing up; this was a new attitude that I was seeing about the time he was a junior in high school. I also knew that this was how he was teaching us to treat him – avoiding him because he didn't choose to speak to us in the morning.

Is this the way he will treat his college roommate or spouse and children someday? How fun is that? Plus, my youngest daughter, Kathy, and I did not deserve to be treated like that (Kelly and Mike had already left for college).

When the children were younger, at our family meetings, we had discussed our "attitude drawer." Explaining to the kids that there will be things that will happen to us during our lifetime which we won't have control over, the only thing we can control is our attitude.

Discussing bad attitudes for not getting to be first, or not having a friend over or not getting to watch more TV, they immediately understood. If the child was pouting or moping around, I would ask them to go to their attitude drawer.

Explaining that each day when you get up in the morning and select your clean underwear for the day, you also get to open your attitude drawer and decide which attitude you will use that day. You always have the right and option to change your attitude at any time. Only you control your attitude.

The kids understood this concept very well and we often teased each other about going to our attitude drawer. I often heard them whispering (just loud enough so they knew I could hear them), as I was leaving the room, "She definitely should have picked a different attitude this morning" or "Do you think she really chose 'that' attitude today?" or "Maybe she only has that one in there – who's going to tell her to look again?" Then more giggling and more whispering.

One day when Nick was in a good mood, I boldly said, "I noticed in the mornings you don't seem to be very happy. I was wondering if the crabby attitude that I've seen in the morning could be put back in the drawer for a day or two and see what else is in there."

Nick was staring at me. How dare I bring up his attitude drawer because he was old enough to figure it out himself. However, he understood what I was saying. Telling him that I was surprised he pushed the good sense of humor attitude to the side and selected instead, Mr. Crabby Pants, which just didn't look that handsome on him, made him smile. He knew it was a point well taken and there wasn't anything else to say.

Believe me, his attitude did not change overnight. He still had that crabby one sometimes, and I would say, "Oh, I see that crabby attitude must have jumped out at you when you opened your attitude drawer this morning. I sure hope you find that funny one soon." He would just ignore me but I knew he had heard what I said.

It wasn't long after that talk when we had come home from a tennis match where Kathy was defeated playing number one singles. When asked if she would like to go out for pizza with Nick and me, she just marched passed us, barked she wasn't hungry and went to her room.

Nick looked at me and quietly said, "I think she's headed straight to her attitude drawer, because she needs to pick out a new one," (as if he was privately coaching her on handling daily activities and attitudes). We both burst out laughing knowing that he was the crabby one and now, the very first time we saw it in his sister, he nailed her on it.

My children were blessed with a great sense of humor, and they used it constantly. We teased about the attitude drawer a lot at our home.

When the children were preparing to go to college, I put our old Victorian home on the market. Working in the yard, I became frustrated as I was trying to do several months of catch-up yard work in one weekend so the yard would look well-tended for the real estate market. Angered with myself that I'd let the yard work get so behind, I now wished I had this gorgeous, thriving garden to complement our home.

When Nick came out of the house, he asked me what was the matter (he could tell by my expression that I wasn't happy). Telling him I was disappointed in myself for letting the planting and weeding of flowers go over the past few months, I was trying to make up for it in a couple of weekends.

He said (in full mockery mode), "Well, we have two choices here; either I can go up to your attitude drawer and look for another one, or you can go, but one of us has to change the one you have, because it's just not that pretty."

We both burst out laughing. We had come full circle.

****

Teaching my children that they were able to choose their attitude for every situation they face was a difficult task, however, it was important because this is a life-long skill. Giving them the responsibility for their own actions, helped them create who they wanted to be.

Chapter 29: Sixteen and Driving (me crazy)

When I was growing up, my dad said to me, "It's your 16th birthday, and you just got your license. Do you want the car tonight to go somewhere with your friends?"

I was ecstatic. How exciting is that? My own dad was giving me permission to be the driver on a night out with my friends. Then I had to ask myself, *Who is this guy and what did they do with my real dad?* My real dad was strict and seemed black and white in his decision-making when I was growing up. This was totally out of character for him to offer me the car. However, I didn't want him to change his mind and quickly yelled out, "Yes!"

I'll never forget his next words, "Well, I want you driving when you are with your friends because you are a good driver." (My head grew a little bigger just hearing that statement, especially since my dad rarely gave us compliments.) "But you have to remember that you are responsible for everyone riding with you. If you are driving recklessly and have an accident and someone is injured or killed, you'll be the one going up to those parents' home and knocking on their door telling them that you were the driver when their son or daughter was injured or killed. Then you tell them why you were driving recklessly. I'll go with you but you'll be the one talking with their parents. Now go on."

What? I felt paralyzed. How could I possibly have fun after he had just dumped the weight of the world on my shoulders? His words echoed in my ears every time someone from the back seat yelled for me to pass a car or race friends driving next to us. His words were etched in stone in my head.

His message worked. I became a very responsible driver.

As I was telling my kids this story, they said, "You'll have to tell us the same thing when we start driving."

I replied, "I don't think you'll want to hear that message."

They assured me they would be ready for that message; however, that was long before they reached driving age. By then it had become known as "the grandpa story." And I was right. They did not want to hear it when they were ready to drive.

Using the same words, the message was, "I would rather have you driving than any of your friends because I know you are a good driver so if you want the car, you have certainly earned the privilege of driving."

Then came the crushing blow. "Do you want to tell the grandpa story or do you want me to tell it?"

Sharing the grandpa story with the teenage drivers that came over to pick up my kids to go out for the night was dreadful for my children. My kids were cringing with embarrassment that I'm even talking with their friends, let alone sharing this story with them.

Sometimes I would ask who in the group was the driver that evening and whoever raised their hand, I'd go over and put my arm around them and say, "You know, Chris, I only have one Nick, and even though he doesn't really like me that much right now, I really like him and I want him home safe and sound tonight. Can you assure me that you'll drive responsibly tonight? Besides, who would pick on Kathy if he's not around?"

Nick's friends willingly played along and said they would personally come over and pick on Kathy (which they already did). And then I would look them in the eyes and say (using that 'I'm holding you accountable' voice), "I'm trusting you with Nick. Can I have your word that you are a careful driver?"

It's empowering to teenagers to accept responsibility. They need to know that they'll be held accountable.

Just as I hated to have my dad say those words to me, I also know he gave me a gift that day to be accountable to myself and everyone else that rode in my car. I passed that gift on to my children (although that's not what they called it at the time).

My kids were always telling me not to say anything to their friends about driving or anything else. Validating how embarrassing this may be to them, I explained it was my responsibility as a parent to have that conversation with whoever is driving. My intention was caring about the safety of the entire group.

They knew I took my role as a parent seriously, which meant I had to be strong enough to step up to the plate when needed. They never doubted that I cared about the safety of all the kids riding with that driver. Their friends knew I cared too. I learned to be strong enough as a parent not to take their words personally.

My kids have already told me that they will use the grandpa story with their children. And their kids will not want to hear it either.

****

Teenage driving is a worry (more like a nightmare!) for all parents, whether your child is the driver or the passenger. It is the parent's responsibility to do everything in our power to make our children safe, accountable and responsible drivers.

Chapter 30: Compassion – Paying It Forward

Your children will see what you're all about by what you live
rather than what you say.   Wayne Dyer

Cars? Who needs 'em? Basically I think cars are just another
way to play havoc with our patience. Just when we think we have
enough money to pay all the bills for the month and we're able to
eek out enough for groceries, something happens to the #!?# car
and the repair bill shows up. And has there ever been a car repair
for $41.37? No, it's $394.12 – always in the hundreds. Whenever we
had car trouble, I knew we were in for more mac and cheese
dinners.

Planting the seed earlier when the kids were ready to drive, I
told them if they wanted their own kids' car, they would have to
help with the expenses. They always agreed but I'm not sure they
knew exactly what that meant. When the time came for discussions
about actually owning a kids' car, we talked and talked some more.
Finally, we all agreed that the kids would pay for their own gas, any
repairs and their own car insurance. I would pay for the car.

Over the years, I had learned that the kids take better care of
something when they have had to spend their own money. All of
those discussions during family meetings were paying off.

When Kelly was a senior in high school, she began working as
a waitress at the country club during the summer, and that too
turned out to be a great experience for both her and the employer.
There was just the problem of getting her back and forth to work.
We definitely needed a second car.

After much car shopping, I purchased a used Ford Escort. It
was the perfect kids' car. We specifically named the car the "Kids
Car" because I didn't want Kelly to think it was only her car and
therefore Mike wouldn't be allowed to drive it when he got his
license, or would have to ask her permission.

We now owned The Bomb (the four door white station wagon with the fake wood paneling which could haul an entire soccer team) and the Kids Car.

Then another incident.

Not too long after we got the Kids Car, Kelly and two of her friends were driving on Interstate 90 to go to the Taste of Chicago and the July 4th fireworks. They were in the center lane of busy I-90 traffic when the engine just died in the Kids Car. (A parent's nightmare.)

As the car came to a stop, Kelly was unable to get the car started again. After stopping traffic in the right lane of I-90, the girls pushed the car over to the side of the road and had the car hood propped up, with none of them knowing what to do next.

Immediately, a car with three teenagers pulled over to help them. (A parent's second nightmare in this story: girls riding in a stranger's car.) Later the girls said the only reason they felt safe getting in the car with the guys is that one of them had braces on his teeth (apparently their thought was that criminals do not shell out the money for braces).

The guys all had on soccer uniforms and said they were on their way to their soccer game. (Obviously, criminals do not wear soccer uniforms to kidnap girls.)

The boys said their uncle owned a car garage and could tow the car that same day. As the story goes, the girls left the Kids Car by the side of the road, went with the guys to call the car garage and made arrangements for the car to be towed.

After the soccer game, the boys drove the girls to the train station, and the girls proceeded to take the train downtown to finish their previously planned evening at the "Taste of Chicago" festival.

The second thing they did not plan on was to miss the last train back home.

Panic began to set in. They called everyone they could think of to come and pick them up; however, no one answered their home phones including myself, as we were driving back from Chicago as well (before cell phones).

The girls finally called Kelly's father (after midnight), who lived in a suburb of Chicago and was fast asleep for the evening. Her dad ended up driving into Chicago and picking the girls up for a very quiet ride back to his home.

The next day Kelly and I made contact with the car garage, and yes, indeed, they had picked up the car. We went the following day to hear the damage. The problem, the garage owner stated, was the engine was without oil. It had seized up, and it would be about $3,000 to put in a rebuilt engine plus any additional parts that he was not able to identify at this time. Since the car was only worth $2,000 when we purchased it, we decided it would not be wise to pour more money into the car.

Kelly paid the $90 towing fee, and we stopped for lunch to discuss our options. Kelly was beside herself and felt terrible that she had wrecked the Kids Car. She couldn't believe I wasn't angry or upset throughout this whole thing. She sheepishly admitted the oil light on the dash had been blinking for awhile but that she ignored it, rather than figure out what to do.

I looked at her and said, "I know we can always buy another car, but I could never, ever buy another Kelly. I could have easily been paying for a funeral if you had an accident on the tollway or someone else may have been injured when they were trying to avoid hitting your car as you were pushing it over to the side of the road. I realize that every kid who drives has some car problem at some point. So I feel very blessed that it is the car that is gone and not you. It's just a piece of metal. And look at all the kids who will learn from this lesson. You have definitely taught all of our family members to always check the oil in their cars. And I learned that I could have been more direct in helping you learn how to take care of the car. We can all learn through this."

We finished our lunch and discussed when we could go car shopping again.

I couldn't believe that she actually owned seeing the flashing oil light on the dash and told me about it. It's that truth thing again – and me not getting angry when she told me the truth – that allowed both of us to solve the problem together.

It was a day I will never forget. Neither will she.

Fast forward several years; Kelly had graduated college and just landed her first job and purchased her first car. It was a beauty. It was a used Honda Accord in perfect condition.

Kelly quickly accepted the responsibility of her new car. She affectionately named her Rhonda Honda. It was two to three months after Kelly purchased her car when her younger brother, Nick, asked to use her car for homecoming. I was shocked that Kelly said, "Yes." Wow. I just imagined he would use the Jetta, which was the replacement for the first kids' car.

This was the beginning of the gifts that I would see first hand. First Kelly had to teach Nick how to drive a stick shift. Then she washed and waxed Rhonda, getting her all ready for the big homecoming dance. I was in awe, watching the magnificent gesture of giving I was seeing between sister and brother.

But it would go far beyond that. Somewhere during the homecoming evening, Nick was backing out of his parking space, and either hit another car or was hit by another car backing out, which caused a scrape in the paint and a small dent to Kelly's car. He said he worried all night knowing he was going to have to tell his sister what had happened to her new car. He hardly slept that night.

In the morning, as soon as she was out of bed, he took her outside to show her what happened. She looked at it and said, "Oh, that's okay, Nick, it's just a piece of metal. It's not really going to show that much anyway. Let's go have breakfast and you can tell me about the dance."

Shock set in. How could she be so relaxed about the damage that had been done to her new car?

She said she remembered the damage she had done to the first kids' car and she knew how upset and anxious Nick must have felt. Kelly also said she remembered how surprised and grateful she felt when she wasn't yelled at, that she had really learned a valuable lesson that day.

I was totally blown away. How powerful to hear how that whole story unfolded. Once again I felt blessed to have seen how love and trust work together and how the things I had taught my children truly affected the people they had become.

****

When an accident or something bad happens, I stand back for a moment and ask myself what I want my children to learn from this or how I would want to be treated if I was the one in trouble. It helped me to decide how I wanted to discuss the situation. I have never learned anything when someone is yelling at me in a rage or shaming me for my behavior. I would never want to treat someone else in that manner. Learning patience, compassion and using open and honest dialogue worked so much better.

Chapter 31: The Kaminskis Hit Broadway

It was Saturday morning, and I received a phone call from my good friend, Ginny, who had two extra tickets to a play in Chicago for that afternoon's performance. Nick, my 17-year-old son, was the only one of the kids home at the time. He was going through the stage best described as "if there was a list of 100 people that he would like to spend time with, my name would appear around the 210th slot – maybe even lower."

Explaining to Nick that Ginny had called with two extra tickets to a play, I asked if he would go with me. He told me that he was going to play pool later with his friends so he would pass on the play tickets.

Pausing for a moment, I then said, "Rarely do I ever force you to do something, but Ginny is offering us something that I can't afford to buy for all four of you children and that's the opportunity to see a play in Chicago and the tickets are probably worth over $100 each. I'm asking you to go with me. I won't accept no for an answer."

Needless to say, Nick was not happy about me forcing him to go to the Chicago theater. He didn't speak to me the entire drive from Woodstock to our friend's home in Barrington. While he was polite and enjoyed conversing with our friends, he didn't speak to me the entire trip to Chicago.

Since Nick and I were seated next to each other during the performance and he had an aisle seat, he had no one else to talk with and the silence was deafening.

Once again, I felt the knot in my stomach. *What on earth was I thinking? Maybe it was a mistake to force Nick to come with me on this trip.* I was doing a pretty good job of beating myself up when the opening scene of "Joseph and the Amazing Technicolor Dreamcoat" began, and I became immersed in the play.

At intermission, Nick leaned over and said to me, "This is good. I'm glad you made me come."

Tears came to my eyes because I thought I had crossed a boundary with him and felt terrible about how I had treated him. He was an adult and I was treating him like a child by forcing him to go to the play. I was so grateful that he was able to enjoy the production, and we both agreed that the music made us want to stand up and belt out a song even though neither one of us can sing.

I continued to pretend that I was sure of myself all along by forcing him to see the play, when inside I was silently so relieved that he was enjoying himself. When the final song ended, Nick leaned over and said, "Do you think it's possible our whole family could see this? That was really good."

And that's how my bank account lost more than $600 to the Chicago theater hosting "Joseph and the Amazing Technicolor Dreamcoat." It was some of the best money I've ever spent as it was wonderful to have our whole family enjoy it together. It was also so incredible that my son, Nick, requested family tickets. Bring on the chicken patties for a few more meals, but it was definitely worth it.

When I told the other kids I had purchased tickets for the play, my oldest son, Mike, said to me, "Someone else can use my ticket because I hate musicals."

Which, of course, made me smile as I replied, "That's exactly what Nick said, however, he is the one that requested we all go as a family, so I am going to ask you to attend this play as well. It's a family function." I wasn't surprised when we received the thumbs up from Mike at intermission. Nick and I smiled at each other knowingly, sharing our inside joke.

One of the most difficult things for me in parenting is — how do you know what is the right decision? Even though my son was 17 at the time, nothing had presented itself like the preceding situation, so I didn't know what the right decision was.

Now I know that next time I would negotiate instead of going right to the force-him-to-go stance. Even though this situation turned out good for all of us, I learned that I didn't feel good forcing

Nick to do something and later apologized to him for my bad judgment. He graciously accepted my apology. Then he apologized for not speaking to me and we both hugged.

Years later, this story unfolded even further. Nick's gift to me for Mother's Day surprised and deeply touched me: he and his fiancée took me to the play "Wicked" in Chicago, followed by a wonderful dinner afterwards.

****

As a parent, you may not always make the "right" decision. Sometimes it will turn out okay, and sometimes you will have to learn from the experience. Decision-making as a parent is a difficult, challenging road. I learned to trust my gut-level feeling – and to apologize when I made mistakes.

Chapter 32: The Best Advice My Mother Gave Me

When Kelly was in her late 20s, she had been trying to encourage me to write about our family for a number of years because she knew that was my dream. She would often send me articles in the mail to read which always motivated me.

Why then, did it take me 10 years to finally begin this book? Oftentimes when I thought about writing a book, it was because I would have loved to read how someone else did this single parenting thing and if it was even possible to survive. Everything I had read previously was written by mothers with one or two children, but never someone who had four. Then I would always ask myself, "Who am I to write a book about parenting?" I certainly didn't have any quick fixes and it wasn't always a pretty picture. Still I wanted to be able to help someone else, knowing if I could have reached out to someone who had been through all of the same issues, I would have felt better. Many of the things we did together worked for our little family of five. I wanted to share that with other parents.

Along with a beautiful article from the May issue of *Real Simple*, honoring Mother's Day, was my daughter's own version of the article, which she called "The Best Advice from My Mom, The Rox," (written, she stated, in no particular order):

1. Stand up for yourself.
2. Love yourself no matter what.
3. Heal yourself first and be whole, before you try to fix your relationships.
4. When you look back on life, you will regret the things you chose NOT to do, instead of the things you did do… so go for it.
5. Always make time for yourself.
6. Treat others as you would want to be treated.
7. I'm worth it!

8. Laughter is the best medicine, and a sense of humor is the first thing to look for in a friend and a partner.
9. It's always okay to cry.
10. Stand up for yourself.
11. The best time to do something nice is when no one else will know.
12. Chicken patties from Market Day can provide months of tasty meals.
13. There is nothing wrong with being alone – it's better to be alone for the right reasons than with someone for the wrong ones.
14. You are the only person responsible for your own happiness.
15. Believe in angels.
16. Stand up for yourself.
17. Honesty is always the best policy.
18. Don't bottle up your feelings – it's always better to talk about them.
19. Brothers and sisters can be more than just siblings; they can be your best friends.
20. Be true to yourself.
21. If someone has the courage to ask for your forgiveness, give it to them.
22. The best you can do is to try your hardest.
23. Sometimes even if you love someone, you have to let them go.
24. Kill 'em with kindness.
25. If you can't be honest with yourself, you can't be honest with anyone.
26. Trust your gut-level reaction.
27. Finish college, no matter what.
28. No truth is worse than a lie, even if that truth is hard to hear.
29. Stand up for yourself.
30. You'll never have time to be friends with everyone, so choose your friends wisely.

31. Being a mom is the most important and most rewarding and most difficult job in the world.
32. Set a good example. (And that's just what you did, Mom!)

Thanks for all you taught me.
Love,
Kelly

****

It sounds like she was listening all along.

Chapter 33: The Best Gift I Gave To Myself

Your kids require you most of all to love them for who they are,
not to spend your whole time trying to correct them.
Bill Ayers

I was so ashamed of being divorced. For the first several years, it was like a huge scarlet letter I wore on my forehead constantly. No matter how hard I tried, I couldn't rub it off.

Divorce brings separation and emotional distance in extended families, as it had mine. I never wanted my children to know the loneliness of not being included by family. Knowing my children have become each other's best friends, all four of them, is comforting going forward, but it wasn't always easy.

One of the biggest factors in creating this friendship and love for each other was learning to listen. Quite often our discussions became a little heated and we each tried to express or defend our opinion a little more clearly by saying basically the same thing a little louder and more enunciated. How novel. And we all did it.

Eventually, if I could see we were headed for a stalemate, I'd ask if we could take a breather and resume our conversation in an hour or maybe even the next day. That would give each of us time to cool down and gave me a chance to remember to listen.

When I listened to what the children were saying and tried to repeat back what was being said, we had more opportunities to successfully negotiate. I became aware that when my children felt heard, they didn't always need to get their own way. They were willing to negotiate. I'm exactly the same way.

If I feel heard, it helps me feel respected.

What I gave my children was the best gift I was able to give: an environment in which they could grow to become best friends with one another forever. What I received in return was their friendship, love and respect – the greatest gift I could ever imagine.

Chapter 34: Moving On

As the children were growing up, there were days that seemed like they'd never end.

There were also days that seemed to fly by.

Overall, I'm so grateful for many things. I'm thankful we listened to each other, gave each other second and third chances (sometimes more), learned to like each other and like ourselves in the process, and most of all, learned to speak from our hearts. I feel very blessed to have learned right beside each of my children and feel honored that we each learned to believe in ourselves and each other and made the choice (repeatedly) to work through our differences.

If you ask them, you'll see a smile come across their face and they'll admit that it wasn't always easy growing up together. However, they'll quickly point out there were many funny, memorable stories that didn't make their way into this book. Fortunately, we learned to laugh at our own mistakes.

We owned them, we embraced them, we learned from them. We shared them many times over. Of course, when we're together, the kids love to share my mistakes more than anyone else's – funny how that happens.

I also feel very blessed that each of the children had the desire and opportunity to continue their education by earning a college degree. They took out college loans and worked while attending classes. Today they each have their own successful careers and have found their niche in the work force that challenges and inspires them.

Me, I have everything I've always wanted and a whole lot more. I had no idea what raising four children as a single parent would be like. Now I know. Was it the most difficult thing I have ever done? Yes. Would I do it over again? In a heartbeat.

Finally, I have learned to listen to my inner voice. By embracing who we are, we open our hearts to others. I'm the person I am today because of all the challenges my children presented to me — they forced me to grow even when I stood with my feet buried in the sand, (maybe concrete on some days) refusing to budge. My inner voice told me to listen to them and walk with them. Their inquisitive minds and ever-present energy kept us moving forward. I will always be thankful to my children for challenging me to become stronger, more motivated and more loving than I thought possible.

Thanks, Kelly, Mike, Nick and Kathy for helping to make me a better me.

I'm still listening and I'm still learning...

* * * * * * * * *

As human beings, our greatness lies not so much in being able to remake the world...as being able to remake ourselves.
Mahatma Gandhi

Epilogue

Kelly's Good-Bye Letter

My daughter, Kelly, owns her own design business in Chicago and wrote me this letter when she was at a conference in Cabo San Lucas during a hurricane which closed the airport, flooded the roads and destroyed many buildings. The hotel where her business conference was held had lost all power and water supply. Many of the windows of the hotel had blown out, and the hotel wing that she was in was evacuated. However, she did not hear the evacuation call and remained in her bathroom, the only place in the hotel room without windows as flying glass and debris were everywhere.

9/21/03

Mom,

I hope this is readable because I'm writing by flashlight in a bathtub at the Hilton in Cabo San Lucas in Mexico. I know I called you earlier to tell you that I wasn't coming home tonight as planned, and now I'm a little afraid that I might not come home at all. I'm scared and I don't know what to do. I thought I would feel better if I wrote to you about how I was feeling and what was going through my mind. I feel very afraid right now but since I started this letter I actually feel a little bit better. I just hope that if something happens to me that this letter finds you so you know that my last thoughts were of you and our family and how loved I feel right now. Before I got in this bathtub I changed into my running clothes in case I have to run somewhere else. No matter where I go, I will take this letter with me in hopes that you get it. I do feel really afraid right now but I don't feel sad. I would be sad if I wasn't proud of my life or if I thought that you and the other kids didn't know how much I love you all. But I am confident that you do know. I am very comforted by that. I am not ready for my life to be over but if it's over, I am proud of who I am and the choices I made. I owe that to you. And to Mike, Nick and Kathy. I am so proud to say that you guys are my family and that I am part of such a unique bond.

I know I tell you all the time that you are the best mom in the whole world but now at this moment I'd like you to know that I really mean it. I feel so lucky that you are my mom and that you have raised me, just like you did, early curfew and all. In all honesty, my real goal in my life is to be like you and raise kids just like you did. I hope in some small ways that I have already become like you and feel so complimented when people say that. You are so amazing and smart and funny and just thinking about you now reminds me that no matter what happens, I have already been the luckiest person in the world just because I'm your daughter. And I'm so lucky that you raised the four of us to be best friends. Mike, Nick and Kathy are so wonderful to me and I am forever grateful. What an incredible gift you gave to all of us.

Please tell Mike that I think he is brilliant and that he is destined for great things if he just believes in himself. He is so smart and so funny and that combination is so rare. Tell him I think he should never doubt himself or what he can do. And also tell him that I'm sorry we're so bad at keeping in touch because he might feel bad about that if something happens to me and I don't want him to. We both know how we feel about each other and there's no amount of time that ever changes that. And tell him to get a cell phone so it doesn't happen with the other kids! Ha-ha!

Tell Nick that he's the best roommate I ever had and I enjoyed every second of living together. Nick has such a great heart and is such a good listener. No wonder he has such loyal, long-time friends. I hope he thinks of me the same way, as one of his best friends, because that's a spot I'd really like to have. Nick is so genuine and so caring – I really admire him for that. He can relate to everyone and make them feel so important, just by being in a conversation with him. That is truly a gift.

Please tell Kathy that she is the best sister I could ever ask for. She should be so proud of who she is because she is truly a beautiful person, inside and out. I think she is going to be the best doctor this world has ever seen. I hope I get to see that. I hope Kathy knows how I feel about her and that I'm so proud to call her my sister and my friend. Kathy will always be a person that other people admire. I know she will use her many gifts to become an amazing person, doctor, mom, friend, and spouse.

All three of them have already become incredible people – siblings that I admire so much and aspire to be like. Mom, you should be so proud that we are all like you. You have given us all the right things to be happy.

152

Please also give my love to Dad, Jean and to April, Jake and Cole. Tell Dad that I'm so grateful for the way our relationship has grown and that I treasure how close we are now. He is a great mentor to me in life and in business and has taught me so much. Tell Jean that she has been a great step-mom to me and an even better friend. Tell Dad and Jean to love and cherish each other. Give giant hugs to April, Jake and Cole – thinking of them now makes me smile. All three of them have brought such joy to my life. I love being their big sister and spending time with them. What a gift they have each been to me, and to our whole family. Tell April, Jake and Cole that they have a special place in my heart and that I'll love them always.

The noises are getting worse and the building is really shaking. I'm not sure what I should do and I feel afraid. Most afraid that I won't see you again or this letter won't reach you somehow. If it doesn't, I think you will already know these things I've written down and that comforts me. I hope you and the kids already know that you have made my life so wonderful and so worthwhile. I have tried to be the best daughter and the best big sister that I can be. I know I've failed sometimes but I have tried my hardest. If something bad does happen, please don't be sad because I don't want you to feel badly – I want you to go on with your lives and continue to touch all the people in your lives. That way I will live on too through you.

I know that all of your angels are with me now and I'm sure they will take care of me forever, even if it is in heaven. Please don't cry or be sad but just know that I am thinking of you all and loving you all so very much.

I have to go so I can save some of my flashlight batteries. I am sending you my love one last time and I will keep you in my heart so that I feel safe.

I love you all so much.
Love,
Kelly

If you find this letter, <u>please</u> give it to:
Roxie Kaminski
(Address)
USA

* * * * *

Kelly hand carried the letter to me one week later. We all celebrated her safe arrival home and listened first-hand to the chilling stories surrounding the hurricane. After reading her letter, I knew that all four kids would continue to surround and support each other through life's joys and struggles.

My job was done.

INDEX

Made in the USA
San Bernardino, CA
21 May 2016